Barbecues

Barbecues

Over 80 recipes for
alfresco eating

hamlyn

First published in Great Britain in 2005 by Hamlyn,
a division of Octopus Publishing Group Ltd,
2–4 Heron Quays, London E14 4JP

ISBN 0 600 61308 9
EAN 9780600613084

A CIP catalogue record for this book is available
from the British Library

Printed and bound in China

10 9 8 7 6 5 4 3 2 1

Notes

Both metric and imperial measurements have
been given in all recipes. Use one set of
measurements only, and not a mixture of both.

Meat and poultry should be cooked thoroughly.
To test if poultry is cooked, pierce the flesh through
the thickest part with a skewer or fork – the juices
should run clear, never pink or red.

This book includes dishes made with nuts and
nut derivatives. It is advisable for those with known
allergic reactions to nuts and nut derivatives and
those who may be potentially vulnerable to these
allergies, such as pregnant and nursing mothers,
invalids, the elderly, babies and children, to avoid
dishes made with nuts and nut oils. It is also
prudent to check the labels of pre-prepared
ingredients for the possible inclusion of nut
derivatives.

The Department of Health advises that eggs should
not be consumed raw. This book contains some
dishes made with raw or lightly cooked eggs. It is
prudent for more vulnerable people, such as
pregnant and nursing mothers, invalids, the elderly,
babies and young children, to avoid uncooked or
lightly cooked dishes made with eggs.

Contents

The great outdoors

Nothing beats the laid-back fun of a summer barbecue – with skewers and steaks sizzling over the coals, big bowls of salad, chunks of crusty bread and jugs of ice-cold drinks. Whether you're enjoying a family get-together, entertaining friends or planning an intimate dinner for two – a barbecue is always the perfect choice.

There's something about the word barbecue that screams 'laid-back, leisurely food and no-fuss fun'. Everyone's always happy to lend a hand when it's needed, and to simply relax in the sun when it's not. Kids love being outside and will have a great time entertaining themselves (as long as they're well away from the cooking area). They'll also have a great appetite – so don't stint on the burgers and sausages. Barbecues are great when the sun goes down too and can be the perfect focus for laid-back entertaining on a balmy summer evening. There's nothing prettier than the flicker of garden candles or tea lights placed in empty jars around the garden while your guests mingle around the barbecue.

PLANNING FOR SUCCESS

There are really only three things you need for a successful barbecue: equipment, the right menu and good weather. A little careful planning is all that's required, and even the most unpredictable element (the weather!) can be made to work.

1 First, you need to make sure you have the right equipment. This means a barbecue, fuel, ignition, tools for cooking and water (in case of emergency).

2 Next, you need the right menu – with drinks, snacks to nibble, food for the barbecue, salads, accompaniments and a dessert.

3 And, finally, you need to check the weather. If it's hot and sunny, make sure there's shade to sit in (as well as plenty of sunscreen and perhaps a few sunhats too!). If it looks as if it might rain, make sure there's comfortable shelter so that everyone can stay dry and still have fun.

CHOOSING THE RIGHT BARBECUE

There are almost as many barbecues to choose from as there are foods to cook on them, and which one to choose can be a mind-boggling affair. Built-in, portable or disposable? Gas-, charcoal- or wood-burning? Large or small? The easiest way to decide is to ask yourself what your own needs are:

• **How often will you use the barbecue?** If, realistically, you're going to have only a couple of barbecues every year, then there's no point in spending a lot of money on a top-of-the-range model. However, if you're going to barbecue every weekend, then it may well be worth investing in a more expensive one that's built to last and fulfils your every need.

• **How big is your garden, and how much storage space do you have?** If you have a small garden, then a small, portable barbecue that can be put away may be the best choice. If you have a bigger garden, then a built-in barbecue can make a great focal point for entertaining and saves the effort of setting up and packing away. If you go for a portable barbecue, check that you have somewhere to store it when it's not in use.

• **How many people will you usually need to cook for?** If you mainly cater for large numbers, then a barbecue with lots of cooking space will be invaluable. However, if you usually cook for just a few people, then a smaller barbecue is more appropriate.

• **Where and when do you want to use it?** Barbecues are great at home, but it can also be fun to take your barbecue on holiday, on a picnic or to the beach. If this sounds like you, then a small, lightweight, easily portable barbecue might be just the thing.

THE BASIC MODELS

There are five main types of barbecue to choose from, and these can vary considerably in size, shape, cost and the fuel they use. Look for models with an adjustable grill rack so you can control the heat more easily.

• **Simple braziers** The simplest type of barbecue available, these consist of a tray on legs in which to place the fuel, with a rack over the top for grilling. They may be near to the ground or high enough to stand over while you cook.

• **Kettle barbecues** These round barbecues have a domed lid, which makes them good for both grilling and roasting. They are good for cooking large pieces of meat or whole fish. There are gas-fuelled and charcoal-burning models.

• **Built-in barbecues** Usually made of brick, these may be freestanding or built into a walled area. Some have a chimney to carry smoke away from the cooking area.

• **Gas barbecues** These are usually constructed like a trolley, with a space for the gas bottle, accessories and work surface. Gas jets heat up ceramic or lava stones in the base of the barbecue, which then throw out heat to cook the food. Look for models with an easy-to-remove tray for catching dripping fat.

• **Disposable barbecues** Cheap to buy for a one-off barbecue, these usually consist of a sturdy foil tray covered with a lightweight rack – with the charcoal already set up for lighting. Once used, they can simply be left to cool and then be thrown away. They are convenient for picnics or camping, and are also useful if you find you need extra grill-space for a large party, or if you are cooking meat and vegetarian foods that need to be kept separate. However, if you plan to use them frequently, it's cheaper to buy a small, lightweight portable brazier.

Barbecue basics

Once you've chosen your barbecue, all you need to do is find the right position, decide which fuel to use, learn how to light it and then get the coals (or gas) to just the right temperature before you start cooking.

THE PERFECT POSITION

Before you light the barbecue, think carefully about where to put it. The position should be safe, sensible, stable and legal.

• **Think about smoke**: don't place the barbecue too close to your house (or your neighbours') or upwind from the eating area.

• **Think about fire**: place the barbecue away from dry plants or wooden fences.

• **Be sure the barbecue is stable** and there is no risk of it getting knocked over.

• **If you are in a public place** check that you are allowed to light a barbecue there.

CHARCOAL, WOOD OR GAS?

Everyone has their own preference for the perfect fuel – and often the type of barbecue you have will dictate which fuel you choose.

• **Charcoal** is cheap and readily available and burns fairly evenly. It comes in two forms: lumpwood or briquettes. Lumpwood charcoal is easier to light than briquettes. Both can be bought in sacks, or in self-lighting packages.

• **Wood** is less predictable to use and it is more difficult to control the heat. You also need to wait for the fuel to burn down to its glowing embers before you can start cooking.

• **Gas** is quick and convenient but does not offer the same flavour as charcoal or wood.

GETTING FIRED UP

With the help of firelighters and/or matches, lighting a barbecue and getting it to just the right temperature is an easy task.

Charcoal: Start at least 30 minutes before you want to start cooking. If you don't have self-lighting bags of charcoal, the easiest way to get the charcoal burning is by using firelighters. Layer the charcoal with firelighters and build a cone-shaped fire in the centre of the barbecue tray. Light the firelighters using a long match, and leave the coals to burn down to ash-coated embers. Spread out the glowing embers into an even layer, then place the grill rack above them and leave it to heat up. If you need to add more coals, add them around the edge of the embers until they warm up, then move them, a few at a time, into the centre of the fire. There should be no flames when you start to cook.

Wood: Start about 1 hour before you want to start cooking, then light the wood in the same way as you would charcoal.

Gas: Start about 15 minutes before you want to start cooking. Switch on the gas and light it, then leave the ceramic or lava rocks to heat up.

PERFECT BARBECUING

Before you start cooking, oil the grill rack using oiled kitchen paper or a basting brush. Cooking times can vary considerably, depending on the heat of the coals, the distance of the rack from the heat and the thickness of the food. However, you can use the following list as a general guideline to how many minutes are needed:

Steaks – *rare:* 3–4; *medium:* 5–6; *well-done:* 8–12

Lamb – *steaks:* 6–8; *cutlets:* 8

Pork – *chops:* 20; *ribs:* 15; *sausages:* 15

Burgers – *thin:* 8–10; *thick:* 12–15

Chicken – *wings:* 8–10; *breasts:* 12; *thighs:* 20; *legs:* 25

Fish fillets – *thin:* 2; *thick:* 6–7

Whole fish – *small:* 6; *medium:* 15; *large:* up to 1 hour (with lid)

Shellfish: *prawns:* 4; *scallops/squid:* 2–3

To assess how hot the coals are, hold your hand a few centimetres/inches above them, and see how long you can keep your hand there:
2 seconds = hot; 3–4 seconds = medium;
5 seconds = low

BARBECUE TOOLS

A few basic tools and accessories will take all the hassle out of cooking on a barbecue. Make sure you've got everything you need before you start putting food on the grill:

• **Long-handled tongs** for turning and lifting food. (Get a second pair for moving coals.)
• **Barbecue trays** for food that is too fragile or too small to cook on the grill.
• **Hinged baskets** for grilling whole fish.
• **Spatula or fish slice** for turning fish, burgers and vegetables.
• **Long-pronged fork** for checking that meat and poultry are cooked at the end of cooking. (Avoid piercing uncooked foods because the juices will run out during cooking, giving dry results.)
• **Pastry brush** for basting food and oiling the grill. (Keep a separate brush for basting raw foods.)
• **Metal and wooden skewers** for making kebabs. (Soak wooden skewers in water for at least 30 minutes before use.)
• **Foil** for wrapping foods before cooking.
• **Wire brush** for cleaning the grill rack.

Fabulous food

The best thing about a barbecue is that almost everything, apart from the actual cooking, can be done in advance. Before you plan the menu, think about the following:

• **How many people have you invited?** This will guide you to the quantity of food and drink needed, and also how many sets of plates, cutlery and glasses you will need. Check that you have enough grill space and fuel to cook the food.

• **Does anyone have special dietary requirements?** If you are catering for a vegetarian or someone with a food allergy, think about whether you will need a separate grill area for their food.

• **How much time do you have for preparation?** This will help you assess the types and numbers of dishes you should prepare. If you're short of time, it might be better to go for a few, simple dishes, whereas if you have a whole day to prepare, you might like to make a number of more complex dishes as well as an impressive dessert.

WHAT KIND OF DISHES?

There's a huge range of delicacies you can cook over a barbecue, from the simplest ready-made sausages and burgers to marinated meat, poultry and fish, and

FOOD SAFETY

When cooking food on a barbecue, always follow the basic rules of food hygiene:

• Always check that pork and poultry are cooked all the way through. Boneless cuts make a good choice because they cook more quickly.

• Never put cooked food on a plate that has held raw meat, poultry or fish.

• Do not baste cooked or nearly cooked food with the same brush that you have used on raw meat, poultry or fish.

• Do not leave food sitting out in the sun: this includes raw meat, poultry and fish, as well as foods such as salads, dips and sauces. Keep them covered in a cool place until you are nearly ready to serve, then uncover them and place them on the table.

mouth-watering vegetarian temptations. You can even barbecue fruits and other sweet foods to make irresistible desserts. (Just flick through the recipes in this book and you'll see how many fabulous ideas there are!)

For a big party, it's great to barbecue a selection of different foods, but you can also cook just one deliciously prepared dish, such as grilled Italian lamb with rosemary oil or stuffed monkfish with balsamic dressing, to great effect. Whatever you decide on, always make a couple of salads and side dishes to accompany the barbecued food, and make sure there's a dessert to follow.

To ensure things run smoothly, offer guests snacks and nibbles while the food cooks. This way, even if you have to wait until the coals are just the right temperature, or the food takes a little longer than expected – your guests won't get hungry or impatient!

CLASSIC GRILLS

Many ingredients can go straight on the grill, while others require a little preparation. Here are just a few of the classic approaches:

• **Straight to the grill** Burgers, sausages and many cuts of meat, poultry and fish can go straight on the grill and are good served with tangy sauces, relishes or salsas (see pages 13–14). Plain grilled fish is often good served with a simple squeeze of lemon juice, or a little garlic or mixed herb butter (see page 15).

• **Marinades and rubs** Meat, poultry, fish, vegetables and other vegetarian foods such as tofu can be given a real flavour boost with a simple marinade (see page 12). Whether it's chunky steaks, delicate shellfish or bite-sized vegetables, marinating for even a short time can transform them.

• **Sizzling kebabs** Cubes of marinated meat, poultry, fish, vegetables and other vegetarian ingredients are delicious threaded on to skewers to make kebabs, and they can be made well in advance. Sweet ingredients such as fruit and marshmallows can also be skewered and grilled to make delicious desserts. Woody herbs and aromatics such as rosemary and lemon grass can be used as skewers to impart extra flavour.

• **Tasty parcels** Both sweet and savoury ingredients can be wrapped up in foil or banana leaves with flavourings, then cooked over the hot coals to give fabulous results.

• **Stuffed and grilled** Ingredients such as veal escalopes and chunky monkfish can be stuffed with a filling, then tied up to make a parcel. These dishes can make an impressive centrepiece for a sophisticated barbecue.

CREATING AN INSTANT BARBECUE

Even with barely an hour or two to prepare, you can still put on a veritable feast if you choose the right dishes. Here are a few ideas for a super-speedy barbecue:

• Offer guests no-fuss nibbles such as crisps and dips when they arrive.

• Go for ready-to-cook and ready-prepared foods such as sausages, burgers, chicken legs or wings, or cubed meat that can quickly be slipped on to skewers with a few bite-sized vegetables.

• Use marinades and spice rubs to add quick-fix flavour. They can be put together in seconds, then left to work their magic.

• Make a no-fuss green salad with prepared salad leaves, cucumber and a splash of ready-made dressing.

• For an almost-instant pasta salad, toss cooked pasta with a jar of marinated vegetables or Italian antipasti. (Drain the vegetables if they're in oil.)

• For a super-speedy potato salad, boil new potatoes until tender, then drain and leave to cool before tossing with mayonnaise, a handful of chopped fresh herbs and a couple of chopped spring onions.

• Buy ready-made sauces and relishes and simply spoon them into serving dishes.

• Don't worry about making a dessert – ice cream or sorbet served with fresh summer berries is a great standby.

Marinades and more

Barbecue marinade
serves **6**
preparation time **5 minutes**

1 teaspoon mustard powder
1 teaspoon salt
½ teaspoon chilli powder
1 tablespoon firmly packed dark brown
  sugar
300 g (10 oz) can condensed tomato soup
2 tablespoons vinegar
2 tablespoons Worcestershire sauce
2 tablespoons soy sauce

1 Mix all the marinade ingredients together
and pour over ribs, chops or chicken to
cover. Leave in a cool place to marinate for
at least 1–2 hours.

Herb marinade
serves **4**
preparation time **5 minutes**

4 tablespoons olive oil
4 garlic cloves, crushed
125 ml (4 fl oz) dry white wine
1 small onion, finely chopped
1 sprig each rosemary, thyme and parsley

1 Mix all the ingredients together and use
to marinate fish, such as tuna or mackerel,
for several hours or overnight.

Sweet and sour marinade
serves **4**
preparation time **5 minutes**

4 tablespoons tomato ketchup
2 tablespoons Worcestershire sauce
2 tablespoons white wine vinegar
2 tablespoons clear honey
2 tablespoons soft brown sugar

1 Mix together all the ingredients. Place
the food in a shallow dish and brush with
the marinade, then cover and refrigerate
for 4 hours, or preferably overnight. This
marinade is perfect for pork spare ribs.

Teriyaki marinade
serves **4**
preparation time **5 minutes**

2 cm (¾ inch) piece of fresh root ginger,
  peeled and finely grated
2 tablespoons soy sauce
1 tablespoon lemon juice
2 tablespoons dry sherry
125 ml (4 fl oz) fish stock

1 In a shallow dish combine all the
ingredients for the marinade. Marinate
the food for at least 30 minutes, turning
occasionally. This is a good marinade for
chicken, salmon and prawns.

Sweetcorn relish

serves **8–10**
preparation time **15 minutes**
cooking time **30 minutes**

4 tablespoons corn oil
2 large onions, finely chopped
1 green pepper, cored, deseeded and finely
 chopped
1 red pepper, cored, deseeded and finely
 chopped
4 celery sticks, finely chopped
1 teaspoon salt
1 large garlic clove, crushed
2 carrots, peeled and cut into small cubes
50 g (2 oz) sugar
2 teaspoons mustard powder
750 g (1½ lb) frozen sweetcorn
450 ml (¾ pint) vinegar

1 Heat the oil in a large pan and add the
onions, peppers and celery. Fry them until
they are soft but not browned, then add the
salt and garlic.

2 Add all the remaining ingredients to the
pan and bring the mixture to the boil.
Reduce the heat and cook, uncovered, for
15 minutes, stirring occasionally.

3 Transfer the relish to a bowl and cool at
room temperature. This relish does not need
time to mature, but if not immediately
consumed, label and store in a cool, dark
place for up to 6 months.

Chermoula

serves **6**
preparation time **10 minutes**

2 teaspoons cumin seeds
1 teaspoon coriander seeds
½ teaspoon crushed dried chillies
3 garlic cloves, crushed
finely grated rind and juice of 1 lime
3 tablespoons olive oil
1 tablespoon chopped mixed coriander
 leaves and parsley
1 teaspoon salt

1 Lightly pound the cumin and coriander
seeds using a pestle and mortar (or a small
bowl and the end of a rolling pin). Mix in a
bowl with the remaining ingredients. Use
chermoula to coat fish before barbecuing.

Basic tomato sauce

serves **4**
preparation time **10 minutes**
cooking time **1 hour**

1 kg (2 lb) fresh ripe tomatoes, quartered
1 onion, finely chopped
2 garlic cloves, chopped
4 basil leaves, bruised
125 ml (4 fl oz) olive oil

1 Place the tomatoes in a large saucepan
with the onion and garlic. Cover the pan,
bring to the boil then cook slowly for
25 minutes. Uncover the pan and simmer
for another 15–30 minutes to evaporate any
extra liquid: the sauce should be quite thick.

2 Purée the sauce in a blender or food
processor, then sieve it to remove any seeds
and skin. Stir in the basil and oil.

Avocado salsa

serves **4**

preparation time **10 minutes**

1 firm, ripe avocado
2 tablespoons lime juice
1 tablespoon finely chopped fresh
   coriander leaves
2 spring onions, finely sliced
salt and freshly ground black pepper
diced red pepper, to garnish

1 Cut lengthways through the avocado as far as the stone, then gently twist the two halves apart. Remove the stone, peel off the skin and cut the avocado into 1-cm (½-inch) dice.

2 Place the avocado flesh in a bowl with the lime juice, coriander and spring onions. Season to taste with salt and pepper and toss lightly to combine. Cover and refrigerate until required. Serve garnished with diced red pepper. This tangy salsa makes a great accompaniment to warm dishes, especially as part of a buffet.

Green mayonnaise

serves **6**

preparation time **10 minutes**

3 egg yolks
1 tablespoon finely chopped chives
1 tablespoon finely chopped parsley
1 tablespoon lemon juice
300 ml (½ pint) olive oil
salt and freshly ground black pepper

1 Place the egg yolks, herbs and lemon juice in a blender or food processor and blend for 1–2 minutes. Keeping the motor running, pour in the oil in a very thin stream until it is all incorporated. Add salt and pepper to taste.

Classic vinaigrette

makes **250 ml (8 fl oz)**

preparation time **5 minutes**

175 ml (6 fl oz) olive oil
4 tablespoons white wine vinegar,
   cider vinegar or tarragon vinegar
1 teaspoon clear honey
2 tablespoons chopped mixed herbs
   (mint, parsley, chives, thyme)
1 garlic clove, crushed
salt and freshly ground black pepper

1 Beat the oil with the vinegar, honey, herbs, garlic and salt and pepper to taste until well blended. Alternatively, place all the ingredients in a screw-top jar and shake vigorously to combine well before using.

Mint dressing

makes **125 ml (4 fl oz)**

preparation time **5 minutes, plus standing**

6 tablespoons olive oil
2 tablespoons lemon juice
2–3 tablespoons chopped mint
pinch of sugar
salt and freshly ground black pepper

1 Beat the oil with the lemon juice, mint, sugar and salt and pepper to taste until well blended, or place all the ingredients in a screw-top jar and shake vigorously to combine well.

2 Set aside for at least 15 minutes to allow the flavours to develop, then beat or shake again and test, before using to dress a cold potato salad or a green leaf salad.

Honey dressing

makes **125 ml (4 fl oz)**
preparation time **5 minutes**

4 tablespoons lemon juice
2 tablespoons clear honey
3 tablespoons olive oil
salt and freshly ground black pepper

1 Beat together the lemon juice, honey, olive oil and salt and pepper to taste until well blended. Alternatively, place all the ingredients in a screw-top jar and shake vigorously to combine well before using to dress green salads.

Mixed herb butter

serves **6**
preparation time **5 minutes,**
plus chilling

75 g (3 oz) butter
½ tablespoon chopped tarragon
½ tablespoon chopped chervil
½ tablespoon chopped dill
½ tablespoon chopped chives
½ tablespoon chopped mint
1 tablespoon lemon juice
salt and freshly ground black pepper

1 Blend the butter in a blender or food processor, then add the rest of the ingredients and mix well. Alternatively, beat the butter in a bowl until creamy, then add the remaining ingredients and combine them.

2 Roll the butter in greaseproof paper to form a sausage shape, then chill until firm. This herb butter can be used with either meat or fish.

Spicy peanut sauce

makes **150 ml (¼ pint)**
preparation time **10 minutes**
cooking time **2 minutes**

50 g (2 oz) creamed coconut
4 tablespoons milk
½ small onion, chopped
1 garlic clove, crushed
4 tablespoons smooth peanut butter
1 teaspoon soft brown sugar
2 teaspoons soy sauce
½ teaspoon ground cumin
½ teaspoon chilli powder
salt and freshly ground black pepper

1 Chop the creamed coconut into pieces and place it in a small pan with the milk. Heat gently for about 2 minutes, stirring constantly, until the coconut melts and forms a paste with the milk.

2 Transfer the coconut mixture to a blender or food processor and add all the remaining ingredients. Process until smooth, then transfer to a small bowl. Cover and set aside until required. It is best to make this rich, spicy dressing in advance to allow the flavours to develop before using it.

Poultry and Game

Versatile poultry,
well-flavoured duck
and robust, meaty
venison are naturals
for the barbecue grill.
Pepped up with
Eastern spices, or
infused with rich
Mediterranean
flavours, the recipes
in this chapter are
sure to tantalize the
tastebuds.

serves **8**
preparation time **30 minutes, plus marinating**
cooking time **12–15 minutes**

Chicken tikka kebabs
with naan bread

1.5 kg (3 lb) skinless, boneless chicken breasts, cut into 2.5 cm (1 inch) cubes
8 naan breads
lemon or lime wedges, to garnish

marinade
2 onions, roughly chopped
5 cm (2 inch) piece of fresh root ginger, peeled and roughly chopped
4 garlic cloves, crushed
300 ml (½ pint) natural yogurt
2 red chillies, deseeded and chopped
1 tablespoon ground coriander
2 teaspoons ground cumin
1 teaspoon turmeric
8 tablespoons lemon juice
2 teaspoons salt

1 To make the marinade, combine all the ingredients in a blender or food processor and process until smooth.

2 Place the chicken cubes in a shallow bowl, pour over the marinade and toss well to coat. Cover the bowl with clingfilm and leave the chicken to marinate in the refrigerator for 8 hours or overnight.

3 Remove the chicken from the marinade with a slotted spoon and pour the marinade into a jug. Thread the chicken on to 16 metal skewers.

4 Cook the kebabs on an oiled barbecue grill over hot coals for 6 minutes on each side, basting frequently with the marinade. Serve the kebabs with warm naan breads and garnish with wedges of lemon or lime.

BARBIE TIP
While the kebabs are cooking, wrap the naan breads in a foil parcel and heat them on the edge of the barbecue grill.

serves **4**
preparation time **25 minutes, plus marinating**
cooking time **11–13 minutes**

Thai chicken skewers
with fiery dipping sauce

4 boneless, skinless chicken
  breasts, about 150 g (5 oz)
  each, cut into thin strips
steamed rice, to serve
coriander sprigs, to garnish

marinade
4 Kaffir lime leaves, shredded
2 lemon grass stalks,
  trimmed of outer leaves
  and thinly sliced
2 garlic cloves, roughly
  chopped
2.5 cm (1 inch) piece of fresh
  root ginger, peeled and
  finely grated
1 fresh red chilli, finely sliced
100 ml (3½ fl oz) peanut oil
3 tablespoons chopped fresh
  coriander leaves
2 tablespoons lime juice
1 tablespoon Thai fish sauce
1 tablespoon light soy sauce

dipping sauce
1 red chilli, deseeded and
  finely chopped
1 Kaffir lime leaf, shredded
200 ml (7 fl oz) coconut milk
2 tablespoons smooth
  peanut butter
1 tablespoon freshly grated
  root ginger
1 tablespoon Thai red curry
  paste
½ tablespoon Thai fish sauce
½ tablespoon soy sauce

1 Mix together all the marinade ingredients in a bowl and add the chicken strips. Cover and chill in the refrigerator for at least 2 hours.

2 Meanwhile, make the dipping sauce. Combine all the ingredients in a small saucepan and simmer gently for about 5 minutes. Keep the sauce warm.

3 Remove the strips of chicken from the marinade and thread them on to 8 pre-soaked wooden skewers in an S-shape. Place on an oiled barbecue grill over medium coals and cook for 6–8 minutes, turning once, until cooked through.

4 Serve the chicken skewers with steamed rice garnished with coriander sprigs. Place the dipping sauce in a bowl or drizzle it over the chicken.

BARBIE TIP
When using wooden skewers, pre-soak them in warm water for at least 30 minutes before using, to avoid them burning over the hot coals.

serves **8**
preparation time **20 minutes, plus marinating**
cooking time **15 minutes**

Chicken skewers
with fruit and nut couscous

1 kg (2 lb) skinless chicken breast fillets
4 tablespoons olive oil
4 garlic cloves, crushed
1 teaspoon ground cumin
1 teaspoon ground turmeric
1 teaspoon paprika
4 teaspoons lemon juice

couscous
8 tablespoons olive oil
2 small onions, finely chopped
2 garlic cloves, crushed
2 teaspoons each ground cumin, cinnamon, pepper and ginger
125 g (4 oz) dried dates, chopped
125 g (4 oz) dried apricots, finely chopped
125 g (4 oz) blanched almonds, toasted and chopped
1.2 litres (2 pints) vegetable stock
375 g (12 oz) couscous
2 tablespoons lemon juice
4 tablespoons chopped fresh coriander leaves
salt and freshly ground black pepper

to garnish
seeds from half a pomegranate
lemon wedges
fresh coriander sprigs

1 Cut the chicken into long thin strips, place them in a shallow dish and add the olive oil, garlic, spices and lemon juice. Stir well, then cover and leave to marinate for 2 hours. Thread the chicken on to 16 pre-soaked wooden skewers.

2 To prepare the fruit and nut mixture, heat half of the oil in a saucepan and fry the onions, garlic and spices for 5 minutes. Stir in the dried fruits and almonds and remove from the heat.

3 Meanwhile, place the couscous in a bowl, pour over the stock, cover with a tea towel and leave for 8–10 minutes, until the grains are fluffed up and the liquid absorbed. Stir in the remaining oil and the fruit and nut mixture, add the lemon juice and coriander and season with salt and pepper to taste.

4 While the couscous is standing, cook the chicken skewers on an oiled barbecue grill over medium coals for 4–5 minutes on each side, until browned and cooked through. Serve with the couscous, garnished with pomegranate seeds, lemon wedges and coriander sprigs.

BARBIE TIP
As an alternative, make the kebabs using large prawns or pieces of vegetable. Marinate and cook in the same way. Prawns will take only 1–2 minutes on each side.

serves **4**
preparation time **15 minutes, plus marinating**
cooking time **about 15 minutes**

Chicken teriyaki
with onion and pepper

**750 g (1½ lb) chicken breast
fillets, cubed
12 spring onions, cut into
5 cm (2 inch) lengths
2 red peppers, cored,
deseeded and cut into
chunks
2 tablespoons vegetable oil
plain boiled rice, to serve**

sauce
**3 tablespoons soy sauce
3 tablespoons honey
3 tablespoons sake or
dry sherry
1 garlic clove, crushed
3 slices of fresh root ginger**

1 Place all the sauce ingredients in a small saucepan, bring to the boil and simmer for 5 minutes until it has thickened. Meanwhile, divide the chicken, spring onions and red peppers between 8 pre-soaked wooden skewers and brush with oil.

2 Place the chicken skewers on an oiled barbecue grill over hot coals and cook for 4 minutes on each side, or until cooked through. Brush with the teriyaki sauce and serve on a bed of plain boiled rice, drizzled with more sauce.

BARBIE TIP
Try to use Japanese-brewed soy sauce, rather than Chinese soy sauce, which has a much saltier, less malty, taste.

serves **4**
preparation time **15–20 minutes**
cooking time **about 10 minutes**

Chicken skewers
with avocado and pistachio salad

4 skinless, boneless chicken breasts, about 150 g (5 oz) each
5 tablespoons extra virgin olive oil
large pinch of Cajun spice mix
1 large ripe avocado, peeled, stoned and diced
2 tablespoons lime juice
40 g (1½ oz) pistachio nuts, roughly chopped
125 g (4 oz) mixed salad leaves
small handful of fresh coriander leaves, torn
salt and freshly ground black pepper

1 Cut the chicken breasts into cubes and thread these on to 8 pre-soaked wooden skewers. Drizzle with a little of the oil, sprinkle with Cajun spice mix and season with salt and pepper. Place the chicken skewers on an oiled barbecue grill over hot coals and cook for 10 minutes, turning once or twice, until browned and cooked through.

2 Meanwhile, place the avocado flesh in a bowl and toss with the lime juice. Add the remaining olive oil and season to taste with salt and pepper. Add the pistachios to the bowl with the salad leaves and torn coriander leaves. Toss together gently, then spoon on to plates and top with the cooked chicken skewers.

serves **4**
preparation time **5 minutes**
cooking time **20–25 minutes**

Barbecued chicken
with lemon and herb marinade

2 garlic cloves, crushed
grated rind and juice of
1 lemon
4 thyme sprigs
6 tablespoons olive oil
1 tablespoon clear honey
1 teaspoon dried oregano
1 teaspoon ground cumin
2 chicken drumsticks
2 chicken thighs
salt and freshly ground
black pepper

1 Place the garlic, lemon rind and juice in a bowl. Add the thyme sprigs, oil, honey, oregano and cumin and season to taste with salt and pepper.

2 Add the chicken portions and stir until well coated.

3 Place the chicken on an oiled barbecue grill and cook over hot coals for 20–25 minutes, turning and basting until browned and cooked through.

BARBIE TIP
Use the same mixture to coat 12 chicken wings, or try turkey portions instead.

serves **8**
preparation time **30 minutes, plus marinating**
cooking time **8–10 minutes**

Cinnamon-spiced chicken wings
with yellow pepper dip

16 large chicken wings
fresh coriander sprigs,
  to garnish

marinade
2 garlic cloves
7 cm (3 inch) piece of fresh root
  ginger, peeled and chopped
juice and finely grated rind
  of 4 limes or 2 lemons
4 tablespoons soy sauce
4 tablespoons groundnut oil
4 teaspoons ground cinnamon
2 teaspoons ground turmeric
4 tablespoons honey
1 teaspoon salt

yellow pepper dip
4 yellow peppers
8 tablespoons natural yogurt
2 tablespoons soy sauce
2 tablespoons chopped fresh
  coriander leaves
freshly ground black pepper

1 Place all the marinade ingredients in a blender or food processor and blend until very smooth. Place the chicken in a bowl, pour over the marinade, toss, cover and leave to marinate for 1–2 hours.

2 To make the yellow pepper dip, place the yellow peppers under a pre-heated grill for about 10 minutes, turning until well charred and blistered all over. Place them in a plastic bag until cool, then peel and deseed them and place the flesh in a blender or food processor with the yogurt; blend until smooth. Pour into a bowl, add the soy sauce and season with pepper; stir in the chopped coriander and set aside.

3 Drain the chicken and cook on an oiled barbecue grill over medium coals for 4–5 minutes on each side, basting with the remaining marinade. Garnish with coriander sprigs and serve with the dip.

BARBIE TIP
Because the chicken wings
are quite small, you can get
plenty of them on the
barbecue grill at the same
time, which makes them
great for large parties.

serves **4**
preparation time **15 minutes, plus marinating**
cooking time **about 25 minutes**

Char-grilled chicken
with coriander salsa

4 skinless chicken breast
fillets, about 200 g (7 oz) each

marinade
2 tablespoons soy sauce
2 teaspoons sesame oil
1 tablespoon olive oil
2 teaspoons clear honey
pinch of dried red chilli flakes

salsa
1 red onion, diced
1 small garlic clove, crushed
1 bunch of fresh coriander
leaves, roughly chopped
6 tablespoons olive oil
grated rind and juice of
1 lemon
1 teaspoon ground cumin
salt and freshly ground black
pepper

to serve
steamed couscous
diced tomato

1 Combine the marinade ingredients in a shallow dish, add the chicken fillets, cover and marinate in the refrigerator for at least 8 hours, but preferably 24 hours.

2 Cook the chicken on an oiled barbecue grill over medium coals for 8 minutes on each side, until browned and cooked through. Wrap them in foil and leave to rest for 5 minutes.

3 Meanwhile, mix all the salsa ingredients together and season with salt and pepper. Set aside to infuse.

4 Strain the marinade juices into a small saucepan and bring to the boil, then remove from the heat but keep warm.

5 Serve the chicken with the couscous tossed with diced tomato and top it with the salsa and the marinade sauce.

> **BARBIE TIP**
> To ensure the chicken is char-grilled on the outside but still moist inside, place it on a hot grill and cook over medium coals.

serves **4**
preparation time **10 minutes**
cooking time **20 minutes**

Crispy duck breasts
with orange and cranberry sauce

2 oranges
125 g (4 oz) cranberries
50 g (2 oz) light brown sugar
1 tablespoon clear honey
4 duck breasts
salt and freshly ground black
pepper

to serve
mashed potato

1 Remove the rind and pith from the oranges and cut them into segments.

2 Place the orange segments, cranberries and sugar in a saucepan with salt and pepper to taste, bring to the boil then simmer until the cranberries are soft. Stir in the honey, and keep warm.

3 Place the duck breasts on an oiled barbecue grill, skin side down, and cook over medium coals for 6–10 minutes, then turn them over and cook on the other side for 4–6 minutes. The skin should be crispy and the flesh tender.

4 Cut the duck into slices and serve with the orange and cranberry sauce. Serve with mashed potato, if liked.

serves **4–6**
preparation time **15 minutes, plus marinating**
cooking time **20 minutes**

Chicken drumsticks
with Jamaican jerk marinade

2 tablespoons sunflower oil
1 small onion, finely chopped
10 allspice berries
2 hot red chillies, deseeded
  and roughly chopped
3 tablespoons lime juice
1 teaspoon salt
12 chicken drumsticks

1 Place all the ingredients, except the chicken drumsticks, in a food processor or spice mill and grind to a paste.

2 Score the chicken drumsticks deeply with a sharp-pointed knife, cutting right down as far as the bone.

3 Coat the chicken with the jerk seasoning mixture, brushing it into the slashes in the meat so that the flavour will penetrate. Cover and marinate in the refrigerator overnight.

4 Place the drumsticks on an oiled barbecue grill over hot coals. Cook, turning frequently, for about 20 minutes, or until the chicken is brown on the outside and no longer pink on the inside. Serve hot, warm or cold, for people to eat with their fingers.

BARBIE TIP
Jerk seasoning can be used with other cuts of chicken, such as thighs or breasts. It is also very good with pork; indeed, jerk pork is one of Jamaica's most famous national dishes.

serves **4**
preparation time **20 minutes**
cooking time **20–25 minutes**

Turkey, tomato and tarragon burgers
with pancetta

8 sun-dried tomato halves in oil, drained and chopped
500 g (1 lb) minced turkey
1 tablespoon chopped tarragon
½ red onion, finely chopped
½ teaspoon paprika
½ teaspoon salt
4 slices smoked pancetta or rindless streaky bacon, halved

to serve
4 ciabatta rolls
shredded radicchio and crisp lettuce

1 Place the sun-dried tomatoes, turkey and tarragon in a blender or food processor and process until smooth. Spoon the mixture into a bowl and stir in the onion. Season with the paprika and salt. Mix well, divide into 4 and shape into burgers. Stretch 2 strips of pancetta over each burger and secure the pancetta with cocktail sticks.

2 Barbecue the burgers over hot coals for 20–25 minutes, turning frequently. Serve at once in the ciabatta rolls with shredded radicchio and lettuce.

BARBIE TIP
Soak the cocktail sticks in water for 30 minutes before use, as you would with wooden skewers, to prevent them burning during cooking.

serves **4**
preparation time **10 minutes**
cooking time **up to 45 minutes**

Loin of venison
with pepper crust

750 g (1½ lb) loin of venison, cut from the haunch
75 g (3 oz) mixed peppercorns, crushed
25 g (1 oz) juniper berries, crushed
½ teaspoon salt
1 egg white, lightly beaten

to serve
green beans
redcurrant jelly
sweet potato chips (optional)

1 Make sure that the venison fits on your barbecue grill; if necessary, cut the loin in half to fit.

2 Mix together the peppercorns, juniper berries and salt, and place in a large shallow dish. Dip the venison into the egg white, then roll it in the peppercorn mixture, covering it evenly all over.

3 Cook the venison on an oiled barbecue grill over hot coals for 4 minutes on each side, turning it carefully so that the crust stays intact. Cook it evenly on all sides, then transfer the loin to a lightly greased roasting tin and cook in a preheated oven, 200°C (400°F) Gas Mark 6, for another 15 minutes for rare, and up to 30 minutes for well done. The exact time depends on the thickness of the loin of venison.

4 Let the venison rest for a few minutes, then slice thickly and serve with green beans, redcurrant jelly and finely sliced sweet potato chips, if liked.

Meat

Sizzling steaks, spicy burgers, sticky spare ribs and juicy lamb cutlets are all classics for the barbecue grill. Whether it's a laid-back barbecue for a Sunday afternoon, or a sophisticated *al fresco* dinner, you're sure to find the perfect recipe among these pages.

serves **2**
preparation time **15 minutes, plus cooling and marinating**
cooking time **about 30 minutes**

Sweet sticky spare ribs
with spicy marinade

1 side pork spare ribs, about 750 g (1½ lb)

marinade
1 small onion, finely chopped
1 garlic clove, crushed
2.5 cm (1 inch) piece of fresh root ginger, peeled and freshly grated
75 ml (3 fl oz) cider vinegar
75 ml (3 fl oz) cola-flavoured drink
2 tablespoons tomato ketchup
1 tablespoon Worcestershire sauce
1 tablespoon soft dark brown sugar
1 tablespoon maple syrup
½ teaspoon Tabasco sauce
½ teaspoon smoked sweet paprika
½ teaspoon oregano
½ teaspoon ground cumin
½ teaspoon ground coriander
salt and freshly ground black pepper

to serve
baked potatoes
homemade coleslaw

1 Place all the marinade ingredients in a small saucepan and heat slowly until just boiling. Reduce the heat and simmer gently for 8–10 minutes, then set aside to cool.

2 Cut the side of pork ribs into 4 pieces and arrange in a large, shallow dish. Pour over the cold marinade, making sure the pork is well coated. Cover and refrigerate for 12 hours or overnight.

3 Place the ribs on an oiled barbecue grill over hot coals. Cook the ribs for about 20 minutes, turning occasionally, until cooked through and sticky. While they are cooking, place the remaining marinade in a small pan on the stove and simmer gently for 10–15 minutes until thick and glossy.

4 Separate the ribs and serve with baked potatoes, homemade coleslaw and the hot marinade.

serves **4**
preparation time **25 minutes**
cooking time **20 minutes**

Pork, prune and leek sausages
with barbecued tomatoes

**150 g (5 oz) leeks, rinsed
and diced
375 g (12 oz) lean minced
pork
50 g (2 oz) millet flakes
100 g (3½ oz) ready-to-eat
stoned prunes, chopped
1 egg yolk
large pinch of ground nutmeg
4 tomatoes, halved
salt and freshly ground
black pepper
sweet potato mash, to serve**

1 Cook the leeks in the top of a steamer for 3 minutes until just tender.

2 Mix the minced pork in a bowl with the millet flakes, prunes, egg yolk, nutmeg and a little salt and pepper, then stir in the leeks.

3 Spoon the mixture into 8 equal mounds on a chopping board then shape each one into a 10 cm (4 inch) long sausage with wetted hands, and place on a barbecue tray.

4 Place the tray on the barbecue grill, and cook for 10 minutes over medium coals, turning the sausages occasionally. Add the tomatoes to the tray and cook for 10 more minutes, until the sausages are golden and the tomatoes hot. Spoon on to plates and serve with sweet potato mash.

BARBIE TIP
Using millet flakes instead of breadcrumbs means that even those people on a gluten-free diet can enjoy a sausage supper. Experiment with your own flavour combinations or add a little crushed juniper, chilli or garlic instead of the nutmeg.

serves **4**
preparation time **15–20 minutes**
cooking time **4–5 minutes**

Veal escalopes
with artichoke paste

125 g (4 oz) bottled globe artichokes in oil, drained, 1 tablespoon oil reserved
4 sun-dried tomato halves in oil, drained
4 veal escalopes, about 125 g (4 oz) each
2 slices prosciutto, halved
4 small mozzarella balls
sunflower oil
salt and freshly ground black pepper
spring onions, to garnish (optional)

1 Place the artichokes, the reserved oil and sun-dried tomatoes in a blender or food processor and process to a smooth paste. Transfer to a bowl and season to taste with salt and pepper.

2 Lay the escalopes between two sheets of lightly oiled clingfilm and pound them with a meat mallet until they are thin but not broken.

3 Spread each escalope with a quarter of the artichoke paste, top with half a slice of prosciutto and a mozzarella ball. Fold the veal over to make a parcel and seal at each end with a cocktail stick.

4 Brush the parcels with oil. Cook on an oiled barbecue grill over hot coals for 4–5 minutes, turning frequently, until the meat is well cooked. Remove the cocktail sticks if you wish and serve immediately. If you like, garnish with spring onions that have been barbecued for a few seconds until wilted.

BARBIE TIP
If you cannot find small mozzarella balls, cut a whole mozzarella cheese into four.

serves **4**
preparation time **10 minutes**
cooking time **about 10 minutes**

Steak and feta burgers
with sun-dried tomatoes

450 g (14½ oz) minced steak
1 tablespoon sun-dried
  tomato paste
2 teaspoons chopped oregano
50 g (2 oz) feta cheese,
  crumbled
1 egg, beaten
4 wholemeal rolls, toasted
1 red onion, sliced
1 small, firm lettuce, leaves
  separated
freshly ground black pepper

1 In a large bowl, mix together the minced steak, tomato paste, oregano and feta. Season well with pepper, and stir through enough beaten egg to bind. Form the mixture into 4 burgers.

2 Place the burgers on an oiled barbecue grill over hot coals and cook for 4–5 minutes on each side, or until browned and cooked through. Make up the burgers in the rolls using the onion and lettuce, and serve with a napkin.

serves **4**
preparation time **10 minutes**
cooking time **6–14 minutes**

Red-hot hamburgers
with spicy greens

Excellent

625 g (1¼ lb) minced beef
2 garlic cloves, crushed
1 red onion, finely chopped
1 red chilli, finely chopped
1 bunch of parsley, chopped
1 tablespoon Worcestershire
** sauce**
1 egg, beaten
4 white or wholemeal
** hamburger buns, split**
spicy greens, such as rocket
** or mizuna**
1 beefsteak tomato, sliced
salt and freshly ground black
** pepper**
sweetcorn relish, to serve
** (see page 13)**

1 Place the minced beef in a large bowl. Add the garlic, red onion, red chilli, parsley, Worcestershire sauce, beaten egg and a little salt and pepper. Mix well.

2 Divide the beef mixture into 4 equal amounts and shape into burgers. Place the burgers on the barbecue grill and cook over hot coals for 3 minutes on each side for rare, 5 minutes for medium or 7 minutes for well done.

3 Toast the bun halves quickly on a clean, hot grill. Fill each bun with some greens, sliced tomato and a grilled burger. Serve with some sweetcorn relish.

BARBIE TIP
These burgers can also be made with minced lamb and served in pitta breads, if preferred.

serves **4**
preparation time **25 minutes, plus cooling and chilling**
cooking time **30–35 minutes**

Beef satay
with Indonesian peanut dipping sauce

500 g (1 lb) beef rump steak

marinade
100 ml (3½ fl oz) coconut milk
2 tablespoons soy sauce
1 red chilli, finely chopped
2 garlic cloves, crushed
grated rind and juice of 1 lime
lime rind, to garnish

Indonesian peanut dipping
sauce
2 tablespoons sunflower oil
1 small onion, finely grated
2 garlic cloves, crushed
2.5 cm (1 inch) piece of fresh
    root ginger, peeled and
    grated
50 g (2 oz) dry roasted
    peanuts, ground in a
    blender or nut mill
large pinch of hot chilli
    powder
½ teaspoon soy sauce
2 tablespoons crunchy
    peanut butter
1–2 tablespoons muscovado
    sugar
2 tablespoons lime juice
200 ml (7 fl oz) carton coconut
    cream

to serve
crisp green salad leaves

1 Cut the beef lengthways into thin strips. Place all the marinade ingredients in a bowl and mix together. Add the beef strips and turn to coat well. Cover and leave to marinate in the refrigerator for at least 4 hours.

2 To make the sauce, heat the oil in a saucepan and gently fry the onion, garlic, ginger and ground peanuts for 10 minutes to develop the flavours. Add the chilli powder, soy sauce, peanut butter, sugar, lime juice and coconut cream, stirring well to combine them. Bring to the boil, then reduce the heat and cook gently for another 10 minutes.

3 Transfer the sauce to a bowl and allow to cool, then cover and chill for at least 30 minutes.

4 Drain the beef, keeping the marinade to one side, then thread the beef in a zig-zag pattern on to 8 pre-soaked wooden skewers. Place the skewers on a lightly oiled barbecue grill and cook over hot coals for 7–8 minutes, or until they are cooked through, turning them and brushing over a little of the marinade from time to time while they are cooking. Serve the beef strips on crisp green salad leaves with some peanut dipping sauce and garnish with strips of lime rind.

BARBIE TIP
In this recipe, the sauce is thicker and richer than the usual satay sauce, so it can be used as a dip. It is delicious with chunky pieces of grilled vegetables and grilled skewered meats, particularly chicken.

serves **4**
preparation time **5 minutes, plus marinating**
cooking time **6–24 minutes**

Sirloin steak
with teriyaki marinade

750 g (1½ lb) thick-cut sirloin steak
stir-fried noodles and vegetables, to serve

teriyaki marinade
100 ml (3½ fl oz) pineapple juice
4 tablespoons soy sauce
2 garlic cloves, crushed
3 cm (1¼ inch) piece of fresh root ginger, peeled and finely chopped

1 Mix together all the ingredients for the marinade. Place the sirloin steak in a shallow dish and cover with the marinade. Turn the steak to coat it well. Cover and refrigerate for 24 hours, turning the meat as frequently as possible.

2 Cook the steak on an oiled barbecue grill over hot coals for 3–4 minutes on each side for rare, 5–6 minutes for medium or 8–12 minutes for well done. Remove when the meat is cooked to your liking.

3 Allow the meat to rest for a few minutes, then slice it thinly. Serve on a bed of stir-fried noodles and vegetables.

BARBIE TIP
Teriyaki is a popular Japanese marinade. The complex flavours of soy sauce and ginger penetrate the meat with very tasty results.

serves **2**
preparation time **30 minutes, plus chilling**
cooking time **15–20 minutes**

Lamb and red bean koftas
with cucumber relish

1 small onion
1 garlic clove, chopped
250 g (8 oz) lean minced lamb
200 g (7 oz) can red kidney
  beans, drained and rinsed
¼ teaspoon ground allspice
3 tablespoons fresh
  breadcrumbs
1 egg yolk
12–16 bay leaves, depending
  on size
olive oil
salt and freshly ground black
  pepper

cucumber relish
5 cm (2 inch) piece of
  cucumber, diced
1 kiwifruit, diced
1 tablespoon chopped mint
few flakes of dried chilli
  (optional)

to serve
4 pitta breads
shredded lettuce
natural yogurt

1 To make the koftas place all the ingredients, except the bay leaves and oil, in a food processor. Season with salt and pepper and blend together. With damp hands, shape into 20 small balls and thread on to 4 metal or pre-soaked wooden skewers. Place on a baking sheet, tuck the bay leaves underneath and between the meatballs and loosely cover with clingfilm, then refrigerate.

2 Mix together the relish ingredients in a small bowl, cover with clingfilm, and refrigerate until required. Brush the koftas with oil and cook on a barbecue grill over hot coals for 12–15 minutes, turning occasionally, until they are browned and cooked through.

3 Sprinkle the pitta breads with water and heat on the barbecue grill until puffy. Make a cut lengthways in the pittas and, discarding the bay leaves, fill with the koftas, lettuce, relish and some yogurt, to serve.

makes **12**
preparation time **10 minutes, plus chilling (optional)**
cooking time **10 minutes**

Sheekh kebabs
with red onions

2 green chillies, deseeded and finely chopped
1 teaspoon grated fresh root ginger
2 garlic cloves, crushed
3 tablespoons chopped fresh coriander leaves
2 tablespoons chopped mint leaves
1 teaspoon cumin seeds
1 tablespoon vegetable oil
½ teaspoon ground cloves
½ teaspoon ground cardamom
500 g (1 lb) minced lamb
salt

to garnish
mint sprigs
lemon wedges

to serve
French bread
red onion, sliced

1 Place the chillies, ginger, garlic, coriander, mint, cumin, oil, ground cloves and cardamom in a food processor or blender and process until fairly smooth. Transfer to a mixing bowl, add the lamb, season with salt and mix well, using your hands. Divide the mixture into 12 portions, then cover and chill for 30 minutes, if time allows.

2 Lightly oil 12 flat metal skewers and mould a sausage-shaped portion of the kebab mixture around each skewer.

3 Place the kebabs on an oiled barbecue grill over hot coals and cook for 3–4 minutes on each side, or until cooked through and browned. Meanwhile, cut diagonal slices from the French loaf and place them on the barbecue grill; cook, turning over halfway, until brown and crispy.

4 Serve the kebabs with the hot French bread and slices of red onion and garnish with mint sprigs and lemon wedges.

BARBIE TIP
The meat mixture can also be formed into balls and threaded on the skewers, perhaps alternating the meatballs with pieces of onion or pepper.

serves **4**
preparation time **20 minutes**
cooking time **10–20 minutes**

Grilled Italian lamb
with rosemary oil

lamb loin roast, about 750 g
 (1½ lb), trimmed of fat
4 garlic cloves, cut into slivers
few small rosemary sprigs
2 red onions, quartered
4 tablespoons olive oil
1 tablespoon chopped
 rosemary
salt and freshly ground black
 pepper

to serve
fresh pasta
Parmesan cheese shavings

1 Make small incisions all over the loin roast and insert the garlic slivers and rosemary sprigs. Place the lamb on an oiled barbecue grill and cook over medium coals, turning occasionally, until browned all over, for about 10 minutes for rare meat, or about 20 minutes for well done. Add the onions to the grill for the last 10 minutes and char on the outside. Let the lamb rest for 5 minutes, then carve into slices.

2 Meanwhile, place the oil and the chopped rosemary in a mortar and crush with a pestle to release the flavours. Season with salt and pepper. Spoon the rosemary oil over the lamb slices and serve at once with the grilled onions. Serve with fresh pasta, lightly tossed in olive oil, and Parmesan shavings.

serves **4**
preparation time **5 minutes, plus marinating**
cooking time **about 1–1¼ hours**

Rosemary and lemon lamb cutlets
with sweet potato skins

4 sweet potatoes
**juice and finely grated rind
of ½ lemon**
1 garlic clove, crushed
**4 rosemary sprigs, finely
chopped**
**4 anchovy fillets in oil,
drained and finely chopped**
2 tablespoons olive oil
2 tablespoons lemon cordial
12 lamb cutlets
**salt and freshly ground black
pepper**
rocket leaves, to garnish

1 Bake the sweet potatoes in a preheated oven, 190°C (375°F), Gas Mark 5, for 45–60 minutes until soft right through. Meanwhile, place the lemon rind and juice in a bowl and add the garlic, rosemary, anchovies, olive oil and lemon cordial. Mix thoroughly and add the lamb cutlets. Season with salt and pepper, turn to coat and set aside to marinate for 15 minutes.

2 Cut the sweet potatoes into quarters, scoop out some of the flesh, brush the skins with oil and season with salt and pepper.

3 Place the lamb and potato skins on an oiled barbecue grill over hot coals, and cook for 3–5 minutes on each side, until the lamb is browned and cooked through. Leave to rest for a few minutes, then serve garnished with rocket leaves.

BARBIE TIP
Trim as much fat as possible off the lamb before cooking. Excess fat will drip down on to the coals and cause flare-ups and burnt food.

serves **6–8**
preparation time **30 minutes, plus soaking**
cooking time **2 hours**

Butterflied leg of lamb
with flageolets and garlic

250 g (8 oz) dried flageolet beans or haricot beans
2 bay leaves
1 large leg of lamb, (approx. 2 kg/4 lb) boned and butterflied
3 tablespoons olive oil
4 whole garlic bulbs
25 g (1 oz) butter
1 large onion
6 celery sticks, cut into 1 cm (½ inch) pieces
25 g (1 oz) mint or parsley leaves
salt and freshly ground black pepper
crusty bread, to serve

1 Place the beans in a bowl with cold water to cover. Soak overnight, then drain, rinse and drain again. Tip the beans into a large saucepan, add the bay leaves and cover with cold water. Bring to the boil, boil rapidly for about 10 minutes, then lower the heat and simmer gently for 50–60 minutes until just tender. Drain the beans well, discarding the bay leaves, then set aside.

2 Remove most of the skin and fat from the lamb, leaving only a thin layer. Brush with the oil and place flat on an oiled barbecue grill over hot coals. Sear the meat for 5–6 minutes on each side, then turn and cook for 10–15 minutes more on each side. About 8–10 minutes before the end of the cooking time, wrap each garlic bulb in a double thickness of foil and place in the embers of the fire to soften the flesh.

3 When the meat is thoroughly cooked, transfer it to a platter, cover with a tent of foil and leave to rest for 10 minutes. Meanwhile, melt the butter in a large saucepan. Add the onion and celery and cook gently for 10–12 minutes, until softened but not coloured. Add the flageolet or haricot beans and heat through, stirring occasionally. Season to taste with salt and pepper, remove from the heat and toss with the mint or parsley leaves.

4 Slice the lamb and serve with the beans. Add some roasted garlic to each portion and offer plenty of crusty bread.

BARBIE TIP
An easy way to barbecue a whole joint like lamb is to remove the bone and flatten it; this speeds up the cooking process. You could do this yourself, or ask your butcher to do it for you.

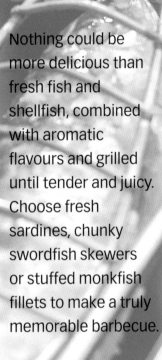

Nothing could be more delicious than fresh fish and shellfish, combined with aromatic flavours and grilled until tender and juicy. Choose fresh sardines, chunky swordfish skewers or stuffed monkfish fillets to make a truly memorable barbecue.

serves **4**
preparation time **10 minutes**
cooking time **15 minutes**

Barbecued snapper
with carrots and caraway seeds

500 g (1 lb) carrots, sliced
2 teaspoons caraway seeds
4 snapper fillets, about
    175 g (6 oz) each
2 oranges
1 handful of fresh coriander
    leaves, roughly chopped,
    plus extra to garnish
4 tablespoons olive oil
salt and freshly ground black
    pepper

1 Place the carrots in a char-grill pan on the hob and cook for 3 minutes on each side, adding the caraway seeds for the last 2 minutes of cooking. Transfer to a bowl and keep warm.

2 Cook the snapper fillets on an oiled barbecue grill over medium coals for 3 minutes on each side.

3 Meanwhile, juice one of the oranges and cut the other into quarters. Place the orange quarters on the barbecue grill until browned.

4 Add the coriander leaves to the carrots and mix well. Season with salt and pepper to taste and stir in the olive oil and orange juice. Serve the cooked fish with the carrots and grilled orange wedges. Garnish with extra chopped coriander.

serves **2**
preparation time **15 minutes**
cooking time **6–8 minutes**

Fresh sardines
with coriander and lime sauce

6 fresh sardines, about 500 g
(1 lb), gutted and descaled
2 limes
4 teaspoons olive oil, plus
extra to grease
15 g (½ oz) fresh coriander
leaves, chopped
salt and freshly ground black
pepper

1 Rinse the fish under cold running water; rub away any remaining scales with your fingertips and check that the insides are clean. Drain the fish, dry them with kitchen paper and place in a hinged barbecue basket designed for fish.

2 Place the basket on the grill rack over hot coals, and cook the sardines for 3 minutes on each side, until they are golden and the flesh flakes easily when pressed with a knife. Transfer the fish to serving plates.

3 Cut one of the limes into wedges and squeeze the juice from the second. Mix the juice, oil, coriander leaves, salt and pepper together and spoon over the sardines. Serve the sardines with the lime wedges.

BARBIE TIP
Sardines are surprisingly cheap to buy and make a nutritious summer supper when served with a green salad and new potatoes.

serves **2**
preparation time **10 minutes**
cooking time **10–15 minutes**

Monkfish brochettes
with cannellini beans and pesto

250 g (8 oz) monkfish, cut
  into 6 pieces
6 Parma ham slices
6 cherry tomatoes
1 yellow pepper, cored,
  deseeded and cut into
  6 pieces
1 tablespoon olive oil
300 g (10 oz) can cannellini
  beans, drained and rinsed
2 tablespoons ready-made
  fresh pesto

1 Wrap each piece of monkfish in a slice of Parma ham.
Thread on to 2 metal or pre-soaked wooden skewers,
alternating with tomatoes and yellow pepper pieces.
Brush the kebabs with the oil and cook on an oiled barbecue
grill over hot coals for 3–4 minutes. Turn and cook for a
further 3 minutes until cooked through.

2 Place the beans in a nonstick saucepan and cook, stirring,
over a low heat for 4–5 minutes, or until hot. Stir in the pesto.
Spoon the beans on to 2 plates, top with the brochettes and
serve immediately.

serves **4**
preparation time **10–15 minutes**
cooking time **20–28 minutes**

Stuffed monkfish
with balsamic dressing

125 ml (4 fl oz) balsamic
  vinegar
4 monkfish fillets, about
  150 g (5 oz) each
4 teaspoons good-quality
  tapenade
8 basil leaves
8 streaky bacon rashers,
  stretched with the back
  of a knife
325 g (11 oz) green beans
200 g (7 oz) frozen peas
6 spring onions, finely sliced
125 g (4 oz) feta cheese,
  crumbled
2 tablespoons basil oil
salt

1 Pour the balsamic vinegar into a small saucepan. Bring
to the boil over a medium heat, then simmer for about
8–10 minutes until thick and glossy. Set aside to cool slightly,
but keep warm.

2 Place the monkfish fillets on a chopping board and, using
a sharp knife, make a deep incision about 5 cm (2 inches) long
in the side of each fillet. Stuff with 1 teaspoon tapenade and
2 basil leaves. Wrap 2 strips of bacon around each fillet,
sealing in the filling. Fasten with pre-soaked cocktail sticks.

3 Bring a saucepan of salted water to the boil, add the green
beans and cook for 5 minutes. Add the peas, bring back to the
boil and cook for another 3 minutes. Drain and keep warm.

4 Place the monkfish directly on an oiled barbecue grill.
Cook over medium coals for 4–5 minutes on each side until
the fish are done. Set aside and leave to rest for a minute
or two.

5 Meanwhile, toss the beans and peas with the spring
onions, feta and basil oil, and arrange on serving plates.
Top with a monkfish fillet (cocktail sticks removed) and serve
immediately, drizzled with the warm balsamic dressing.

serves **4**
preparation time **20 minutes, plus marinating**
cooking time **15–20 minutes**

Monkfish fillets
with garlic and rosemary

500 g (1 lb) ripe tomatoes, skinned
1 tablespoon balsamic vinegar
2 monkfish fillets, about 375 g (12 oz) each, skinned
4 garlic cloves, cut into thin slivers
2 long rosemary sprigs
5 tablespoons olive oil
1 tablespoon lemon juice
salt and freshly ground black pepper
crusty bread, to serve

1 Place the tomatoes in a blender or food processor and process until smooth. Strain through a sieve into a bowl, season to taste with the vinegar, salt and pepper, then cover and set aside.

2 Slice each monkfish fillet lengthways, almost but not quite all the way through, to make a pocket. Lay the garlic slivers down the length of the pocket in each fillet and top with a rosemary sprig. Add salt and pepper to taste. Re-form both fillets and tie them with string at 2 cm (¾ inch) intervals.

3 Mix the olive oil and lemon juice in a shallow dish, large enough to hold both fillets. Add the monkfish, spoon the oil and lemon juice over the top, then cover. Marinate for 1 hour, turning occasionally.

4 Drain the monkfish and cook on an oiled barbecue grill over medium coals for 15–20 minutes, turning and basting frequently, until the flesh is opaque and just cooked. Meanwhile, pour the tomato sauce into a small saucepan and heat through. Remove the string and slice the fish thinly. Serve with the tomato sauce and some good crusty bread.

BARBIE TIP
Rosemary is a very pungent herb. Here, the monkfish fillets are stuffed with sharpened rosemary sprigs with the leaves removed, so the aroma permeates the fish without being overwhelming.

serves **4**
preparation time **20 minutes, plus marinating**
cooking time **5–6 minutes**

Mediterranean swordfish skewers
with peppers and mango

**500 g (1 lb) swordfish steak,
skinned and cut into large
cubes**
**1 green pepper, cored,
deseeded and cut into
2.5 cm (1 inch) pieces**
**1 red pepper, cored,
deseeded and cut into
2.5 cm (1 inch) pieces**
1 red onion, cut into quarters
**1 ripe but firm mango, peeled
and cut into thick slices**

marinade
2–3 thyme sprigs
**leaves from 1–2 rosemary
sprigs**
grated rind of 1 lemon
1 garlic clove, lightly crushed
8 tablespoons olive oil
2 teaspoons fennel seeds
freshly ground black pepper

fennel and olive salad
**1 large fennel bulb, sliced
very finely**
**100 g (3½ oz) good-quality
Kalamata olives, pitted**
grated rind of 1 lemon
**2 tablespoons extra virgin
olive oil**
1 tablespoon lemon juice
**salt and freshly ground black
pepper**
fennel fronds, to garnish

1 Mix together all the marinade ingredients and place in a large, shallow dish with the swordfish cubes, peppers, onion and mango. Cover and set aside at room temperature for about 1 hour.

2 Arrange the fennel slices on a large serving plate and scatter with the olives and lemon rind.

3 Thread the swordfish, peppers, onion and mango on to metal or pre-soaked wooden skewers. Place the skewers directly on the oiled barbecue grill and cook over medium coals for about 5 minutes, turning occasionally, until the fish is thoroughly cooked.

4 Drizzle the olive oil and lemon juice over the fennel salad and scatter with the fennel fronds. Season well with salt and pepper and serve immediately with the swordfish skewers.

serves **4**
preparation time **5 minutes, plus chilling**
cooking time **6–8 minutes**

Swordfish steaks
with mustard and chive butter

100 g (3½ oz) butter, softened
2 tablespoons finely snipped chives
1 tablespoon prepared English mustard
4 swordfish steaks or fillets, about 200 g (7 oz) each
4 tablespoons lemon juice
salt and freshly ground black pepper

to garnish
whole chives
lemon wedges

to serve
cherry tomato salad
new potatoes or boiled rice

1 In a small bowl, mix the butter, chives and mustard. Turn the butter on to a piece of greaseproof paper and press it into a sausage shape. Wrap the paper around the butter, twist the ends and roll the butter into a neat sausage, then chill it in the freezer for 10–15 minutes or until firm.

2 Lay the swordfish on an oiled barbecue grill and sprinkle with lemon juice. Season the fish well with salt and pepper and grill over hot coals for 6–8 minutes or until cooked through, when the fish will flake easily.

3 While the fish is grilling, remove the butter from the freezer and cut it into slices. Transfer the fish to warmed serving plates and top with the butter. Garnish with chives and lemon wedges and serve at once. A cherry tomato salad and new potatoes or boiled rice go well with the fish.

BARBIE TIP
Mahi mahi and halibut are particularly good in place of the swordfish as they are also firm and flavoursome.

serves **4**
preparation time **15 minutes**
cooking time **3–4 minutes, plus resting**

Spiced swordfish
with fennel and mint salad

2 **teaspoons crushed coriander seeds**
4 **swordfish steaks, about 200 g (7 oz) each**
4–6 **tablespoons extra virgin olive oil**
1 **large fennel bulb, trimmed**
1 **garlic clove, thinly sliced**
2 **tablespoons baby capers in salt, rinsed**
handful of mint leaves
1–2 **tablespoons lemon juice**
salt and freshly ground black pepper
rocket leaves, to serve

1 Combine the coriander seeds with some salt and pepper. Brush the swordfish fillets with a little of the oil and rub with the spice mix. Set aside until ready to cook.

2 Discard the tough outer layer of fennel, cut the bulb in half lengthways and then crossways, into wafer-thin slices. Place in a bowl with the garlic, capers, mint leaves, the remaining oil and lemon juice. Season with salt and pepper.

3 Cook the swordfish steaks on an oiled barbecue grill over hot coals for 1½ minutes on each side, then wrap them in foil and leave to rest for 5 minutes. Serve the swordfish and any juices with the fennel salad and rocket.

BARBIE TIP
Swordfish is a wonderfully meaty fish that requires only a short cooking time; if you overcook it, it can become dry and tough. As with meat, allowing the fish to rest before eating it maximizes its moistness and tenderness.

serves **4**
preparation time **15 minutes, plus cooling and chilling**
cooking time **20 minutes**

Fresh tuna steaks
with sweetcorn and avocado salsa

4 tuna steaks, about 175 g (6 oz) each

salsa
2 sweetcorn cobs, stripped of husks and threads
3 tablespoons extra virgin olive oil
1 tablespoon finely chopped red onion
3–4 tablespoons lime juice
2 dashes of jalapeño sauce
1 small red chilli, deseeded and finely chopped
¼ small red pepper, cored, deseeded and finely chopped
1 large firm, red plum tomato, skinned, deseeded and finely chopped
¼ teaspoon ground coriander
2 tablespoons finely chopped fresh coriander leaves
1 firm, ripe avocado, halved, stoned, peeled and chopped
salt and freshly ground black pepper

1 To make the salsa, plunge the sweetcorn cobs into a saucepan of boiling water, return to the boil and blanch for 3–4 minutes. Drain, rub with a little of the olive oil, and place on an oiled barbecue grill over hot coals for 10–15 minutes, turning occasionally, until tender and well toasted. Leave to cool slightly, then scrape the kernels into a bowl and set aside to cool.

2 Add the onion to the corn with the lime juice, jalapeño sauce, chilli, red pepper, tomato, ground and chopped coriander, the remaining oil and salt and pepper. Toss gently to combine, then fold in the avocado. Taste and adjust the seasoning as necessary. Cover and chill for at least 30 minutes for the flavours to develop.

3 Brush the tuna steaks with a little of the olive oil. Cook on an oiled barbecue grill over hot coals for 2 minutes on each side. Serve with the salsa.

serves **4**
preparation time **15 minutes, plus marinating**
cooking time **6–8 minutes**

Miso-grilled salmon kebabs
with cucumber salad

2 tablespoons soy sauce
2 tablespoons sake or dry
   sherry
2 tablespoons clear honey
2 tablespoons miso paste
4 skinless salmon fillets,
   about 200 g (7 oz) each,
   cut into cubes
2 small cucumbers, deseeded
   and sliced
1 red bird's eye chilli,
   deseeded and finely
   chopped
plain boiled rice, to serve

dressing
3 tablespoons rice wine
   vinegar
3 tablespoons caster sugar
3 tablespoons water
½ teaspoon salt

1 Stir together the soy sauce, sake or sherry, honey and miso paste until smooth then pour into a shallow dish. Add the salmon fillets, cover and marinate in the refrigerator for 4 hours, or preferably overnight.

2 Meanwhile, combine the dressing ingredients in a small saucepan and heat gently to dissolve the sugar, then set aside to cool. Mix in the cucumbers and chilli.

3 Thread the cubes of salmon on to 4 pre-soaked wooden skewers. Cook on an oiled barbecue grill over hot coals for 3–4 minutes on each side until the fish is browned and cooked through. Serve with the cucumber salad and some boiled rice.

BARBIE TIP
There are several different varieties of miso paste, each with its own distinct flavour. Choose red or brown miso for this dish, rather than the milder, sweeter white paste.

serves **4**
preparation time **10 minutes, plus marinating**
cooking time **15–20 minutes**

Grilled miso cod
with bok choy

**4 chunky cod fillets, about
175 g (6 oz) each
4 heads bok choy, halved
lengthways
olive oil**

miso sauce
**100 g (3½ oz) miso paste
4 tablespoons soy sauce
4 tablespoons sake
4 tablespoons rice wine
(mirin)
4 tablespoons caster sugar**

1 First make the miso sauce. Place the miso paste, soy sauce, sake, rice wine and sugar in a small saucepan and heat gently until the sugar has dissolved. Simmer very gently for about 5 minutes, stirring frequently. Remove from the heat and set aside to cool.

2 Arrange the cod fillets in a snug-fitting dish and cover with the cold miso sauce. Rub the sauce over the fillets so that they are completely covered and leave to marinate for at least 6 hours, but preferably overnight.

3 Bring a saucepan of water to the boil, then plunge in the bok choy and blanch for 1–2 minutes, then drain. Brush a little oil over the cut side of the bok choy.

4 Remove the cod fillets from the miso sauce and place them on an oiled barbecue grill. Cook for 2–3 minutes over medium heat, then carefully turn them over and cook for an additional 2–3 minutes until they are cooked through. When you turn the cod over, add the bok choy, cut-side down, and cook for about 2 minutes until hot and lightly browned. Remove the cod and bok choy, arrange on a serving plate and serve immediately.

serves **4**
preparation time **10 minutes, plus marinating**
cooking time **4–6 minutes**

Mediterranean prawns
with spicy marinade

**500 g (1 lb) raw tiger prawns,
in their shells
4 tablespoons olive oil
2 garlic cloves, finely crushed
1 teaspoon ground cumin
½ teaspoon ground ginger
1 teaspoon paprika
¼ teaspoon cayenne pepper
handful of fresh coriander
leaves, finely chopped
salt
lemon wedges, to serve**

1 Peel and devein most of the prawns, leaving a few whole, since they look so attractive.

2 Mix the olive oil, garlic, cumin, ginger, paprika, cayenne pepper and coriander in a bowl. Add the prawns and toss to combine. Season with salt and leave to marinate while you light the barbecue.

3 Divide the prawns between four metal or pre-soaked wooden skewers. Place them on an oiled barbecue grill and cook them over medium coals for 2–3 minutes on each side until they are thoroughly cooked. Serve hot, accompanied by lemon wedges.

serves **2**
preparation time **20 minutes, plus time to prepare the lobster**
cooking time **10 minutes**

Garlicky lobster
with lemon butter and mayonnaise

**1 steamed lobster, 1–1½ kg
(2–3 lb)
75 g (3 oz) butter, at room
temperature
1 garlic clove, crushed
1 tablespoon capers in
sea salt, rinsed and drained
1 tablespoon lemon juice
1 tablespoon chopped chervil
1 tablespoon chopped
flat-leaf parsley
1 teaspoon chopped tarragon**

mayonnaise
**2 egg yolks, at room
temperature
pinch of salt
150 ml (¼ pint) peanut oil
300 ml (½ pint) mild extra
virgin olive oil
1 tablespoon lemon juice
1 teaspoon wholegrain
mustard
salt and freshly ground black
pepper**

1 Using a very sharp knife, cut the lobster in half lengthways and remove the intestinal vein that runs down the back. Crack the claws and set aside.

2 To make the mayonnaise, place the egg yolks in a bowl with a pinch of salt and whisk (an electric mixer fitted with a whisk attachment works best) for 1 minute until the eggs are frothy. Very slowly, add the peanut oil drop by drop until you have a thick glossy mixture. Now do the same with the olive oil, whisking continuously until all the oil has been incorporated. Still whisking, drizzle in the lemon juice and the mustard. Season with salt and pepper to taste.

3 Mix 25 g (1 oz) of the butter with the garlic and smear the lobster flesh with the garlicky butter. Lay the shell side of the lobster on an oiled barbecue grill and cook over medium coals for 3–4 minutes, then turn it on to the cut side and cook for about 2 minutes until the flesh and claws are hot and browned. Remove from the barbecue and keep warm while you prepare the lemon butter.

4 Melt the remaining butter in a small pan and heat until it begins to turn golden and smells nutty. Stir in the capers, lemon juice and herbs, then remove from the heat.

5 Serve the lobster halves with the lemon caper butter and a small dish of the homemade mayonnaise.

BARBIE TIP
You can buy ready-cooked lobsters from a fishmonger or some supermarkets, but langoustines and tiger prawns also work very well.

From divine vegetable accompaniments to irresistible meals for the vegetarian, this chapter is packed with inspired ideas for meat-free dishes. Choose a selection of dishes to create a feast that will appeal to vegetarians and meat-eaters alike.

Vegetables and Vegetarian

serves **4**
preparation time **25 minutes**
cooking time **30 minutes**

Vegetable kebabs
with spicy peanut sauce

2 tablespoons lime juice
1 tablespoon blackstrap
  molasses
1 tablespoon soy sauce
1 tablespoon sweet
  chilli sauce
1 tablespoon olive oil
125 g (4 oz) tofu, cubed
1 cooking apple, quartered
4 pineapple chunks
4 mango chunks
4 tomatoes, halved
  horizontally
1 red onion, quartered
8 mushrooms, halved
1 red pepper, cored, deseeded
  and quartered
1 green pepper, cored,
  deseeded and quartered
1 sweetcorn cob, cooked and
  sliced into 8 rounds
1 sweet potato, boiled and
  thickly sliced
1 courgette, thickly sliced
250 ml (8 fl oz) spicy peanut
  sauce (see page 15)
boiled brown basmati rice or
  stir-fried rice noodles,
  to serve

to garnish
lime wedges
sprinkling of grated coconut
  and chopped fresh
  coriander leaves

1 Pour the lime juice, molasses, soy sauce, sweet chilli sauce and oil into a large bowl and mix well. Add the tofu and all the prepared fruit and vegetables, and stir until thoroughly coated.

2 Thread chunks of fruit and vegetables on to 8 pre-soaked wooden skewers, alternating ingredients to give a range of colour and texture. Place on an oiled barbecue grill and cook over medium coals for 8–10 minutes until browned on all sides.

3 Serve the kebabs on a bed of brown basmati rice or stir-fried rice noodles with the peanut sauce poured over the top. Garnish each serving with a wedge of lime and a sprinkling of grated coconut and chopped coriander.

serves **4**
preparation time **10–15 minutes, plus chilling**
cooking time **20–25 minutes**

Potato wedges
with hot tomato salsa

4 large potatoes
4 tablespoons olive oil
salad leaves, to serve

hot tomato salsa
1 small red onion, finely
chopped
1 garlic clove, finely chopped
500 g (1 lb) sweet ripe
tomatoes, skinned,
deseeded and chopped
1–2 moderately hot red
chillies, deseeded and
finely chopped
3 tablespoons finely chopped
fresh coriander leaves
1 tablespoon finely chopped
parsley
1 tablespoon lime juice
3 tablespoons extra virgin
olive oil
pinch of sugar
salt and freshly ground black
pepper
salad leaves, to serve

1 To prepare the tomato salsa, place the onion, garlic, tomatoes and chillies in a bowl. Add the coriander and parsley and stir in the lime juice and olive oil. Season with a pinch of sugar and salt and pepper and mix lightly.

2 Cover and chill for 30–60 minutes, to give the flavours time to develop.

3 Place the whole, unpeeled potatoes in a large pan of cold water, bring to the boil, reduce the heat and simmer for 15–20 minutes or until just tender. Drain, and when cool enough to handle, cut each potato into large wedges.

4 Brush the potatoes wedges with the oil and lay on an oiled barbecue grill. Cook over hot coals for 5–6 minutes, turning frequently, until golden brown. Serve with the tomato salsa and some salad leaves.

serves **4**
preparation time **15 minutes**
cooking time **10 minutes**

Nut koftas
with minted yogurt

5–6 tablespoons vegetable oil
1 onion, chopped
½ teaspoon crushed chilli flakes
2 garlic cloves, roughly chopped
1 tablespoon medium curry paste
425 g (14 oz) can cannellini beans, rinsed and drained
175 g (6 oz) ground almonds
75 g (3 oz) chopped honey-roasted or salted almonds
1 egg
200 ml (7 fl oz) natural yogurt
2 tablespoons chopped mint
1 tablespoon lemon juice
salt and freshly ground black pepper
warm naan bread, to serve
salad leaves, to garnish

1 Heat 3 tablespoons of the oil in a frying pan, add the onion and fry for 4 minutes. Add the chilli flakes, garlic and curry paste and fry for a further 1 minute.

2 Transfer to a food processor or blender with the beans, ground almonds, chopped almonds, egg and a little salt and pepper, and process until the mixture starts to bind together.

3 With lightly floured hands, take about one-eighth of the mixture and mould it around a pre-soaked wooden skewer, forming it into a sausage about 2.5 cm (1 inch) thick. Make 7 more koftas in the same way. Place the skewers on an oiled barbecue grill over medium coals and brush with another tablespoon of the oil. Cook for about 5 minutes, until golden, turning once.

4 Meanwhile, mix together the yogurt and mint in a small serving bowl and season to taste with salt and pepper. In a separate bowl, mix together the remaining oil, lemon juice and a little salt and pepper.

5 Brush the koftas with the lemon dressing and serve with the yogurt dressing on warm naan bread garnished with salad leaves.

BARBIE TIP
Be sure to oil the barbecue rack well before you place the koftas on it. They are a little crumbly and may be difficult to turn if they stick.

serves 4
preparation time **10 minutes**
cooking time **10 minutes**

Bean and pepper cakes
with lemon mayonnaise

75 g (3 oz) green beans,
    roughly chopped
2 tablespoons groundnut or
    vegetable oil, plus extra
    for frying
1 red pepper, cored, deseeded
    and diced
4 garlic cloves, crushed
2 teaspoons mild chilli powder
425 g (14 oz) can red kidney
    beans, rinsed and drained
75 g (3 oz) fresh white
    breadcrumbs
1 egg yolk
salt and freshly ground black
    pepper

lemon mayonnaise
4 tablespoons mayonnaise
finely grated rind of 1 lemon
1 teaspoon lemon juice

1 Blanch the green beans in a pan of lightly salted boiling water for 1–2 minutes, or until softened. Drain. Meanwhile, heat the groundnut or vegetable oil in a frying pan and add the red pepper, garlic and chilli powder. Cook for 2 minutes.

2 Transfer the mixture to a blender or food processor and add the red kidney beans, breadcrumbs and egg yolk. Process very briefly until the ingredients are roughly chopped. Add the drained green beans and season to taste with salt and pepper. Process until the ingredients are just combined.

3 Turn the mixture into a bowl and divide it into 8 portions. Using lightly floured hands, shape the portions into little cakes. Mix the mayonnaise with the lemon rind and juice and season to taste with salt and pepper. Set aside.

4 Heat the oil for frying in a large frying pan and cook the cakes for about 3 minutes on each side until crisp and golden. Serve with the lemon mayonnaise.

BARBIE TIP
These crisp bean cakes, packed into warm pitta breads and served with a salad, make a fairly substantial lunch or supper dish. Any unbaked cakes, interleaved with waxed paper, will keep in the refrigerator for a day or so.

serves **4**
preparation time **15 minutes**
cooking time **5–6 minutes**

Barbecued asparagus
with balsamic tomato dressing

2 tablespoons balsamic
   vinegar
1–2 garlic cloves, crushed
375 g (12 oz) tomatoes,
   skinned, deseeded and
   chopped
7 tablespoons extra virgin
   olive oil
500 g (1 lb) young asparagus
   spears
50 g (2 oz) pine nuts, toasted
25 g (1 oz) Parmesan cheese,
   shaved into thin slivers
sea salt flakes and freshly
   ground black pepper
warm bread, to serve

1 Place the vinegar, garlic, chopped tomatoes and 5 tablespoons of the olive oil in a small bowl. Mix well to combine and set aside.

2 Trim the asparagus spears to remove any tough, fibrous stems. Brush the asparagus with the remaining olive oil and cook on an oiled barbecue grill over medium coals for 5–6 minutes until tender.

3 Divide the asparagus between 4 warmed serving plates. Spoon over the balsamic vinegar and tomato dressing, top with the pine nuts and Parmesan slivers and sprinkle with the sea salt flakes and pepper. Serve at once with plenty of warm bread to mop up the juices.

BARBIE TIP
Plainly grilled, asparagus is delicious served with fish, poultry or meat.

serves **4**
preparation time **10 minutes, plus setting**
cooking time **10–15 minutes**

Parmesan and herb polenta wedges
with tomato and mint salsa

600 ml (1 pint) water
150 g (5 oz) quick-cooking polenta
75 g (3 oz) butter
100 g (3½ oz) Parmesan cheese, freshly grated
2 tablespoons chopped chives
2 tablespoons roughly chopped parsley
2 tablespoons chopped chervil
salt and freshly ground black pepper

spicy cherry tomato salsa
300 g (10 oz) ripe cherry tomatoes, quartered
2 small red chillies, deseeded and finely chopped
1 small red onion, finely chopped
2 tablespoons chilli oil
2 tablespoons extra virgin olive oil
2 tablespoons lime juice
2 tablespoons shredded mint

1 Bring the measured water to a simmer in a saucepan, pour in the polenta and beat well with a wooden spoon until it is thick and smooth. Reduce the heat and continue stirring for about 5 minutes (or according to the packet instructions) to cook the polenta.

2 Remove the pan from the heat and add the butter, Parmesan, chives, parsley and chervil and stir until well combined. Season with salt and pepper then turn into a greased 25 cm (10 inch) cake tin, at least 2.5 cm (1 inch) deep. Smooth the top with the back of a spoon and allow to set for about 5–10 minutes.

3 Combine all the salsa ingredients in a bowl and season with salt and pepper to taste. Set aside.

4 Carefully remove the set polenta from the cake tin, transfer it to a chopping board, and cut it into 8 wedges.

5 Place the polenta wedges in a barbecue tray, and place this on a barbecue grill. Cook over medium coals for 2–3 minutes on each side, until heated through and golden. Serve 2 wedges per person with a spoonful of the salsa on the side.

serves **4**
preparation time **10 minutes, plus marinating**
cooking time **about 8 minutes**

Grilled thyme-marinated goats' cheeses
with walnut bread

4 crottins de chèvre, or small, firm goats' cheeses, halved vertically
4 slices walnut bread

marinade
200 ml (7 fl oz) olive oil, plus extra if necessary
50 ml (2 fl oz) walnut oil
1 teaspoon dried thyme or lemon thyme sprigs
grated rind of 1 lemon
1 teaspoon dried chilli flakes
1 small garlic clove, thinly sliced
8 black peppercorns
8 large vine leaves in brine, rinsed well in cold water

to serve
green salad
balsamic vinegar

1 Place all the marinade ingredients in a 500 ml (17 fl oz) screw-top jar and mix well. Add the halved goats' cheeses and leave to marinate in a cool place for at least 24 hours and up to 3 days.

2 Remove the cheeses from the marinade and drain on kitchen paper to remove any excess oil. Place the vine leaves on a chopping board and place half a goats' cheese in the centre of each one. Wrap the leaves around the cheese so that it is sealed inside.

3 Place the walnut bread on an oiled barbecue grill and cook over medium coals for 2 minutes. Keep the bread warm. Place the 8 leaf parcels (seam side down) and the tomato halves on the barbecue grill and cook for 8 minutes, turning once, until the leaves are crispy and the cheese is melting and the tomatoes are soft.

4 Serve the goats' cheeses immediately with the grilled walnut bread and a little green salad, drizzled with the marinating oil and some balsamic vinegar.

serves **4**
preparation time **15 minutes**
cooking time **30–40 minutes**

Sweetcorn cobs
with skorthalia

4 whole sweetcorn cobs,
  with husks

skorthalia
50 g (2 oz) fresh white
  breadcrumbs
75 g (3 oz) ground almonds
4 garlic cloves, crushed
2 tablespoons lemon juice
150 ml (¼ pint) olive oil
salt and freshly ground black
  pepper

1 To make the skorthalia, place the breadcrumbs in a bowl and cover with water. Soak for 5 minutes, then squeeze out the excess liquid and place the crumbs in a blender or food processor. Add the ground almonds, garlic and 1 tablespoon of the lemon juice, and process until well mixed. With the motor running, gradually add the olive oil in a thin, steady stream until the mixture resembles mayonnaise. Add more lemon juice and salt and pepper to taste.

2 Pull down the husks of the sweetcorn cobs and remove the inner skins. Pull the husks back over the corn cobs. Place on an oiled barbecue grill over hot coals and cook for 30–40 minutes, until the kernels are juicy and come away easily from the core.

3 To serve, pull back the husks of the corn cobs and spread with the skorthalia.

BARBIE TIP
Skorthalia is a garlic sauce that can also be served with other vegetables, or grilled meat or fish. It goes particularly well with barbecued courgettes and fennel wedges.

Salads

No barbecue is complete without a selection of fabulous salads. Try tangy Watermelon and Feta Salad with robust meaty grills, or wholesome Roasted Vegetable and Bean Salad with spicy skewers and char-grilled chicken.

serves **4**
preparation time **15 minutes, plus resting**
cooking time **10 minutes**

Warm tea-smoked salmon salad
with wilted rocket

4 salmon fillets, about 125 g
  (4 oz) each
125 g (4 oz) cherry tomatoes,
  halved
125 g (4 oz) rocket

smoke mix
8 tablespoons Jasmine tea
  leaves
8 tablespoons soft brown sugar
8 tablespoons long-grain rice

dressing
1 shallot, finely chopped
1 garlic clove, finely chopped
few thyme leaves
1 teaspoon Dijon mustard
2 teaspoons white wine
  vinegar
4–5 tablespoons extra virgin
  olive oil
salt and freshly ground black
  pepper

1 Mix together all the ingredients for the smoke mix. Line a wok with a large sheet of foil, allowing it to overhang the edges, and pour in the smoke mix. Place a trivet over the top. Cover with a tight-fitting lid and heat for 5 minutes or until the mixture is smoking.

2 Meanwhile, remove any bones from the salmon with tweezers. Place the tomatoes in a bowl with the rocket.

3 Quickly remove the lid from the wok and place the salmon fillets, skin-side down, on the trivet. Cover and cook over a high heat for 5 minutes. Remove from the heat and set aside, covered, for another 3 minutes.

4 Meanwhile, make the dressing. Place the shallot, garlic, thyme leaves, mustard, vinegar and oil in a bowl, and season to taste with salt and pepper. Whisk thoroughly to combine.

5 Flake the salmon into the salad, add the dressing and toss well. Serve immediately.

BARBIE TIP
Smoking fish and meat over a mixture of tea leaves, sugar and rice is a method widely used in Chinese cooking, but this dish adapts the method for European tastes.

serves **4**
preparation time **10–15 minutes**
cooking time **5–6 minutes**

Smoked chicken and avocado salad
with tarragon and mustard dressing

6 tablespoons olive oil
4 slices of day-old bread,
cut into 1 cm (½ inch) dice
500 g (1 lb) smoked chicken
breast slices
3 small crisp lettuces or
lettuce hearts
1 large ripe avocado, peeled,
stoned and diced
25 g (1 oz) freshly grated
Parmesan cheese

dressing
125 ml (4 fl oz) extra virgin
olive oil
2 tablespoons tarragon
vinegar
1 tablespoon wholegrain
mustard
1 tablespoon chopped
tarragon
1 teaspoon caster sugar
salt and freshly ground black
pepper

1 To make the croûtons, heat the oil in a frying pan and fry the bread cubes, stirring constantly, for 5–6 minutes until golden on all sides. Drain on kitchen paper.

2 Cut the chicken breast slices into bite-sized pieces and place in a large bowl. Add the lettuce leaves to the chicken with the avocado, croûtons and Parmesan.

3 Whisk the dressing ingredients together and season with salt and pepper. Pour the dressing over the salad and toss well until the salad is evenly coated. Serve at once.

> **BARBIE TIP**
> Because smoked chicken is hot-smoked, it is already cooked and ready to eat. You can take advantage of such tasty cooked ingredients to throw together salads in minutes.

Orange and avocado salad
with spicy citrus dressing

4 large juicy oranges
2 small ripe avocados, peeled
and stoned
2 teaspoons cardamom pods
3 tablespoons extra virgin
olive oil
1 tablespoon clear honey
pinch of ground allspice
2 teaspoons lemon juice
salt and freshly ground black
pepper
watercress sprigs, to garnish

1 Cut the skin and the white membrane off the oranges. Working over a bowl to catch the juice, cut between the membranes to remove the segments; reserve the juice. Slice the avocados and toss gently with the orange segments. Pile on to serving plates.

2 Reserve a few whole cardamom pods for garnishing. Crush the remainder to extract the seeds, using a mortar and pestle or a small bowl and the end of a rolling pin. Pick out and discard the pods.

3 Mix the seeds with the oil, honey, allspice, lemon juice, salt and pepper to taste and the reserved orange juice. Garnish the salad with the watercress sprigs and reserved cardamom pods and serve with the dressing spooned over the top.

Fig, mozzarella and prosciutto salad
with verjuice dressing

8–12 ripe black figs
250 g (8 oz) buffalo mozzarella
8 prosciutto slices
a few basil leaves

dressing
3 tablespoons extra virgin
  olive oil
1 tablespoon verjuice
salt and freshly ground black
  pepper

1 Cut the figs into quarters, tear the mozzarella and prosciutto into bite-sized pieces and arrange on a large platter with the basil leaves.

2 Whisk together the extra virgin olive oil, verjuice and salt and pepper to taste. Drizzle the dressing over the salad and serve at once.

BARBIE TIP
Verjuice, made from unripe grapes, has a strong, acidic flavour and is used in cooking as an alternative to lemon juice or vinegar. It gives the dressing a lovely flavour. If you cannot find it, use a good-quality white wine vinegar sweetened with a pinch of sugar instead.

serves **4**
preparation time **10 minutes**
cooking time **2 minutes**

Watermelon and feta salad
with fruity dressing

1 tablespoon black sesame
  seeds
500 g (1 lb) watermelon,
  peeled, deseeded and diced
175 g (6 oz) feta cheese, diced
50 g (2 oz) rocket leaves
handful of mint, parsley and
  coriander sprigs
6 tablespoons extra virgin
  olive oil
1 tablespoon orange flower
  water
1½ tablespoons lemon juice
1 teaspoon pomegranate
  syrup (optional)
½ teaspoon sugar
salt and freshly ground black
  pepper
toasted pitta breads, to serve
  (optional)

1 Dry-fry the sesame seeds for a few minutes until aromatic, then set aside. Arrange the watermelon and feta on a large plate with the rocket and herbs.

2 Whisk together the oil, orange flower water, lemon juice, pomegranate syrup, if using, and sugar, then season to taste with salt and pepper. Drizzle the dressing over the salad, scatter with the sesame seeds, and serve with toasted pitta breads, if liked.

serves **4**
preparation time **15 minutes**
cooking time **up to 40 minutes**

Roasted vegetable and bean salad
with herb vinaigrette

1 aubergine
1 red pepper, halved, cored
  and deseeded
1 yellow pepper, halved,
  cored and deseeded
1 courgette
4 garlic cloves
4 tablespoons olive oil
1 teaspoon coarse sea salt
300 g (10 oz) cooked
  flageolet beans
2 tablespoons chopped
  mixed herbs (parsley,
  oregano or coriander
  and mint)
6 tablespoons Classic
  vinaigrette (see page 14)
pepper
mint leaves, to garnish

1 Cut all the vegetables into strips and put them into a roasting tin. Add the garlic cloves. Sprinkle over the olive oil, salt and some pepper.

2 Place the tin in a preheated oven, 220°C (425°F), Gas Mark 7, and roast for up to 40 minutes, or until the vegetables are cooked. Transfer the vegetables to a shallow bowl and leave to cool.

3 Add the beans and toss lightly. Stir the herbs into the vinaigrette, pour it over the salad and serve garnished with the mint leaves.

BARBIE TIP
Other vegetables, including fennel, tomatoes, baby squash and mild chillies, would also work well in this salad.

serves **4**
preparation time **10 minutes, plus cooling**
cooking time **15 minutes**

Bulgar wheat salad
with fennel, orange and spinach

150 g (5 oz) bulgar wheat
1 tablespoon olive oil
2 fennel bulbs, finely sliced
175 g (6 oz) baby spinach
  leaves
3 oranges, segmented
2 tablespoons pumpkin
  seeds, toasted

dressing
4 tablespoons natural yogurt
2 tablespoons chopped fresh
  coriander leaves
½ small cucumber, finely
  chopped
1 tablespoon extra virgin olive
  oil
salt and freshly ground black
  pepper

1 Prepare the bulgar wheat according to the packet instructions. Set aside to cool. Heat the oil in a frying pan, add the fennel and fry for 8–10 minutes until tender and browned. Add the spinach to the pan and stir through until it is just wilted.

2 Toss the fennel and spinach mixture with the bulgar wheat, then add the orange segments and pumpkin seeds.

3 Mix all the dressing ingredients together, stir through the salad and serve.

makes **350 ml (12 fl oz)**
preparation time **10 minutes, plus chilling**

Onion and tomato salsa
with coriander

1 red onion, finely chopped
425 g (14 oz) small vine-
  ripened tomatoes, halved,
  deseeded and chopped
2 garlic cloves, crushed
15 g (½ oz) chopped coriander
  leaves
salt and freshly ground black
  pepper

1 Place the red onion, tomatoes, garlic and coriander leaves in a bowl and mix together. Season lightly with salt and pepper, then cover and chill for at least 30 minutes for the flavours to develop.

BARBIE TIP
Serve with cold meats or as a side dish with curries and other spicy foods.

serves **2**
preparation time **10 minutes**
cooking time **10–12 minutes**

Mixed bean and chorizo salad
with lemon dressing

75 g (3 oz) fresh or frozen green beans
200 g (7 oz) frozen baby broad beans
100 g (3½ oz) chorizo sausage, diced
½ small red onion, finely chopped
3 tablespoons chopped parsley
salt and freshly ground black pepper
wholemeal bread, to serve

dressing
2 tablespoons extra virgin olive oil
juice of half lemon
1 garlic clove, crushed (optional)

1 Plunge the green and broad beans into a saucepan of boiling water and cook for 3 minutes, or until tender. Drain, rinse under cold running water, drain again, then cut the green beans into 3 pieces.

2 Place the chorizo in a frying pan and cook over a high heat for 6–8 minutes, turning occasionally, until browned and piping hot. Set aside.

3 To make the dressing, mix together the oil, lemon juice and garlic, if using, in a salad bowl. Season to taste with salt and pepper and add the green and broad beans, the chorizo, onion and parsley, then toss together. Serve with warmed wholemeal bread.

BARBIE TIP
Quick and easy to prepare, this salad makes a great supper dish and any leftovers can be stored in a small container in the refrigerator and used next day.

Desserts

Whether it's a Classic Lemon Tart that you've made in advance, or some Barbecued Honeyed Peaches to cook over the fading embers of the barbecue, this chapter is packed with mouth-watering desserts to make an impressive end to the perfect barbecue.

serves **4**

preparation time **15–20 minutes, plus chilling**

Summer fruit skewers
with banana fromage frais

4 thin lemon grass stalks

400 g (13 oz) strawberries, rinsed and halved

3 nectarines or peaches, rinsed, halved, stoned and thickly sliced

4 kiwifruit, peeled and thickly sliced

grated rind and juice of 1 lime

1 banana

200 g (7 oz) virtually fat-free fromage frais

1 Cut the lemon grass stalks in half lengthways and peel off the outer grubby leaves. Using the clean stalks as skewers, thread strawberries, nectarines and kiwifruit alternately on to the lemon grass until all the stalks have been filled. Place them on a plate and drizzle the lime juice over the fruit. Chill until needed.

2 Just before serving, mash the banana with a fork, then stir it into the fromage frais with the lime rind. Spoon the sauce into a small bowl and serve with the fruit skewers.

BARBIE TIP
Since banana discolours with standing, the sauce is best made just before serving or no more than 30 minutes in advance.

serves **4**
preparation time **5 minutes**
cooking time **10 minutes**

Barbecued figs
with yogurt and honey

8 ripe figs
4 tablespoons natural yogurt
2 tablespoons clear honey

1 Wrap each fig in a parcel of double-thickness foil and place on a barbecue grill. Cook over medium coals for 8 minutes, turning occasionally, until the figs are hot and slightly soft. Remove them, unwrap them and cut in half.

2 Arrange the figs on 4 plates and serve with a spoonful of natural yogurt and some honey spooned over the top.

serves **4**
preparation time **5 minutes**
cooking time **10–12 minutes**

Blackened bananas
with mascarpone and rum cream

1–2 tablespoons caster sugar
½ teaspoon ground cinnamon
2 teaspoons rum
250 g (8 oz) mascarpone cheese
8 small bananas

1 Mix the sugar, cinnamon and rum in a bowl. Stir in the mascarpone, mix well and set aside.

2 Place the whole, unpeeled bananas on a barbecue grill over hot coals and cook for 10–12 minutes, turning the bananas as the skins darken, until they are black all over and the flesh is very tender.

3 To serve, split the bananas open and spread the flesh with the mascarpone cream.

BARBIE TIP
If you don't have any mascarpone cheese, simply serve the bananas with some whipped cream.

serves **6**
preparation time **15 minutes, plus freezing**

Strawberry ice cream
with wild strawberries

500 g (1 lb) strawberries, hulled
4 tablespoons fresh orange juice
175 g (6 oz) caster sugar
450 ml (¾ pint) whipping cream

to decorate (optional)
wild strawberries
strawberry syrup

1 Finely mash the strawberries and mix with the orange juice to form a smooth purée. Stir in the sugar.

2 Whip the cream until it forms soft peaks and fold it into the purée. Pour the mixture into a 1 kg (2 lb) loaf tin. Freeze for 1½ hours or until partly frozen.

3 Turn the mixture into a bowl, break it up with a fork and then whisk until smooth. Return the mixture to the loaf tin and freeze for at least 5 hours until completely frozen.

4 Transfer the ice cream to the refrigerator 30 minutes before serving, to soften. Decorate with wild strawberries and strawberry syrup, if liked.

BARBIE TIP
If using an ice cream maker, follow the recipe until the end of step 1. Place the mixture in the machine and add the cream. Churn and freeze following the manufacturer's instructions.

serves **2**
preparation time **5 minutes, plus chilling**
cooking time **5 minutes**

Summer fruit compôte
with Greek yogurt

250 g (8 oz) mixed summer fruit (raspberries, blueberries and strawberries), thawed if frozen
finely grated rind and juice of 1 large orange
1 tablespoon redcurrant jelly
250 ml (8 fl oz) Greek yogurt, to serve

1 Place the fruit, orange rind and juice and redcurrant jelly in a large saucepan. Cover and cook gently for 5 minutes, or until the juices flow and the fruit is softened. Remove from the heat and set aside.

2 Chill the fruit compôte for at least 1 hour. Serve with spoonfuls of Greek yogurt.

serves **4**
preparation time **10 minutes**
cooking time **14 minutes**

Panettone and peaches
with sweet mascarpone

4 slices of panettone (Italian yeast cake)
4 peaches, halved and stoned
50 g (2 oz) ground almonds
25 g (1 oz) soft brown sugar
200 ml (7 fl oz) mascarpone cheese
clear honey, for drizzling

1 Toast the panettone slices on an oiled barbecued grill over medium coals for 4 minutes on each side. Remove and keep warm.

2 Cut the peach halves into wedges and cook them on the barbecue grill for 3 minutes on each side. Meanwhile, mix the ground almonds with the sugar and mascarpone to get a marbled effect.

3 Divide the peach wedges between the toasted panettone slices. To serve, add a generous spoonful of the mascarpone mixture and drizzle honey over the peaches.

BARBIE TIP
Although a traditional Italian Christmas treat, panettone is available throughout the year, but if you can't find it, try brioche bread as an alternative.

serves **4**
preparation time **15 minutes**
cooking time **12–15 minutes**

Barbecued honeyed peaches
with amaretti

4 ripe peaches
300 ml (½ pint) Marsala
4 tablespoons clear honey
1 strip of orange rind
25 g (1 oz) butter, melted
4 amaretti biscuits
vanilla ice cream or
crème fraîche, to serve

1 Cut a small cross in the top and bottom of each peach and place them in a pan of boiling water, leave for 20 seconds, then transfer with a slotted spoon to a bowl of cold water. Peel the peaches, cut them in half lengthways and remove the stones.

2 Place the Marsala, honey and orange rind in a large saucepan, bring to the boil, then simmer for 2 minutes. Add the peach halves and simmer for 3–4 minutes until they are just tender. Remove the pan from the heat and leave the peaches to cool in the syrup.

3 Remove the peaches with a slotted spoon and place the remaining syrup in a small saucepan. Bring to the boil and reduce by half.

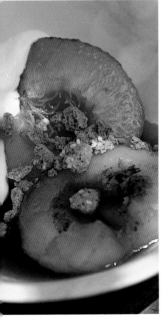

4 Brush the peaches with the melted butter and place them on an oiled barbecue grill over medium coals for 5–7 minutes, turning once.

5 Transfer the hot peaches to serving plates, spoon over a little of the reduced syrup and crumble over the amaretti biscuits. Serve with vanilla ice cream or crème fraîche.

> **BARBIE TIP**
> Use very ripe peaches because they have the best flavour, but be careful when turning them, since they will be soft.

serves **4**
preparation time **10 minutes, plus infusing and standing**
cooking time **about 1 hour**

Baked lemon custards
with bay leaves

12 fresh bay leaves, bruised
2 tablespoons finely grated
lemon rind
150 ml (¼ pint) double cream
4 eggs, plus 1 egg yolk
150 g (5 oz) caster sugar
100 ml (3½ fl oz) lemon juice
bay leaves, to decorate

1 Place the bay leaves, lemon rind and cream in a small saucepan and heat gently until it reaches boiling point. Remove from the heat and set aside for 2 hours to infuse.

2 Whisk together the eggs, egg yolk and sugar until the mixture is pale and creamy, then whisk in the lemon juice. Strain the cream mixture through a fine strainer into the egg mixture and stir until combined.

3 Pour the custard into 4 individual ramekins and place on a baking sheet. Bake in a preheated oven, 120°C (250°F), Gas Mark ½, for 50 minutes, or until the custards are almost set in the middle. Leave to stand until cold and then chill until required. Let the custards return to room temperature before serving. Decorate with bay leaves.

serves **8**
preparation time **20 minutes, plus chilling**
cooking time **40–45 minutes**

Uncooked lime cheesecake
with strawberries and blueberries

50 g (2 oz) butter
2 tablespoons golden syrup
150 g (5 oz) malted milk
  biscuits, crushed

filling
250 g (8 oz) mascarpone
  cheese
200 g (7 oz) virtually fat-free
  fromage frais
50 g (2 oz) caster sugar, sifted
grated rind and juice of
  2 limes
150 ml (¼ pint) double cream

to decorate
250 g (8 oz) strawberries,
  halved or sliced, if large
125 g (4 oz) fresh blueberries
icing sugar, sifted (optional)

1 To make the base, melt the butter and syrup in a saucepan. Place the biscuits in a plastic bag, crush finely with a rolling pin, then stir into the butter mixture. Mix well and press into the base of an 18 cm (7 inch) loose-bottomed, fluted flan tin.

2 Beat the mascarpone cheese in a bowl to soften it, then stir in the fromage frais, sugar and lime rind. Gradually beat in the lime juice.

3 In a second, smaller bowl, whisk the cream until it forms soft peaks, then fold it into the mascarpone mixture. Spoon the creamy filling on to the biscuit base and swirl the top with the back of a spoon.

4 Chill the cheesecake in the refrigerate for 3 hours or longer, if preferred. To serve, carefully remove the cheesecake from the tin and decorate with berries and a dusting of icing sugar, if liked.

serves **4**
preparation time **25 minutes, plus freezing**
cooking time **4–5 minutes**

Lime and mango granita

50 g (2 oz) caster sugar
300 ml (½ pint) water
**finely grated rind and juice of
2 limes**
1 large ripe mango
**sliced mango, to decorate
(optional)**

1 Place the sugar, water and lime rind in a small saucepan and heat gently for 4–5 minutes until the sugar has completely dissolved. Leave to cool.

2 Cut a thick slice off either side of the mango to reveal the large flat stone, then make criss-cross cuts in these slices and scoop the flesh away from the skin, using a spoon. Cut away the flesh surrounding the stone and remove the skin. Process the mango flesh in a blender or food processor until smooth.

3 Mix together the mango purée, sugar syrup and lime juice, then pour it into a shallow metal dish so that it is about 2 cm (¾ inch) deep. Freeze for 1 hour.

4 Take the dish out of the freezer and mash the mixture with a fork to break up any large ice crystals. Return to the freezer and freeze for 1½ hours, beating the mixture with a fork at 30 minute intervals until the granita has the consistency of crushed ice.

5 Spoon the granita into 4 dishes and decorate with extra slices of mango, if liked. Transfer any remaining granita to a plastic container with a lid and return to the freezer.

BARBIE TIP
A can of mango in fruit juice makes a good alternative to fresh mango. Purée the fruit with the juice and add to the sugar syrup and lime juice.

serves **8**
preparation time **15 minutes**
cooking time **25–30 minutes**

Black Forest chocolate cake
with chocolate sauce

250 g (8 oz) self-raising wholemeal flour
250 g (8 oz) soft brown sugar
2 tablespoons cocoa powder
2 heaped teaspoons carob powder
125 ml (4 fl oz) sunflower oil
150 ml (¼ pint) milk
1 tablespoon natural yogurt or coconut cream
1 dessertspoon cider vinegar
pinch of salt
25 g (1 oz) dark chocolate (70 per cent cocoa solids)
fresh cherries or berries, to decorate
hot chocolate sauce, to serve

filling
4 tablespoons cream cheese
1 teaspoon lime rind
4 tablespoons morello cherry or blackberry jam

sauce
200 g (7 oz) dark chocolate, broken into pieces
4 tablespoons milk
3 tablespoons golden syrup
½ teaspoon vanilla essence
25 g (1 oz) unsalted butter

1 Oil two 20 cm (8 inch) circular sponge tins and line them with nonstick baking paper.

2 Place all the cake ingredients, except the chocolate, in a food processor and beat together thoroughly.

3 Coarsely grate or chop the chocolate and add to the cake mixture. Divide the mixture between the sponge tins and level the tops with a spatula.

4 Bake the sponges in a preheated oven, 180°C (350°F), Gas Mark 4, for 25–30 minutes, or until a cocktail stick inserted into the centre of each sponge comes out clean. Allow to cool a little, then turn out on to a wire rack and leave until completely cold.

5 To make the sauce, put the chocolate, milk, golden syrup and vanilla essence into a small, heavy-based saucepan and heat gently, stirring frequently, until the chocolate has melted. Stir in the butter. Continue stirring until the sauce is smooth, then pour it into a jug.

6 Place the cream cheese in a bowl and stir in the lime rind. Spread one side of a cold sponge with the lime cream cheese, and spread the other sponge with jam. Sandwich them together and place on a serving plate.

7 Pour over the thick chocolate sauce and decorate the cake with fresh cherries or berries.

serves **8**
preparation time **20 minutes, plus chilling**
cooking time **40–45 minutes**

Classic lemon tart

200 g (7 oz) plain flour
½ teaspoon salt
100 g (3½ oz) chilled butter,
    diced
2 tablespoons icing sugar, plus
    extra for dusting
2 egg yolks
1–2 teaspoons cold water

filling
3 eggs, plus 1 egg yolk
450 ml (¾ pint) double cream
125 g (4 oz) caster sugar
150 ml (¼ pint) lemon juice

1 Place the flour in a bowl, add the salt and diced butter, and rub in with the fingertips until the mixture resembles fine breadcrumbs. Stir in the sugar and gradually work in the egg yolk and measured water to make a firm dough.

2 Knead the dough briefly on a lightly floured surface, then cover with clingfilm and chill for 30 minutes. Roll out the dough and use it to line a 25 cm (10 inch) fluted flan tin. Prick the pastry shell with a fork and chill for 20 minutes.

3 Line the pastry shell with nonstick baking paper, fill with baking beans and cook in a preheated oven, 200°C (400°F), Gas Mark 6, for 10 minutes. Remove the paper and beans and bake for a further 10 minutes until crisp and golden. Remove from the oven and reduce the temperature to 150°C (300°F), Gas Mark 2.

4 Beat together all the filling ingredients, pour them into the pastry shell and bake for 20–25 minutes, or until the filling is just set. Leave the tart to cool completely, dust with icing sugar and serve.

Index

Acknowledgements

Executive Editor Nicky Hill
Project Editor Jessica Cowie

Executive Art Editor Tokiko Morishima
Designer Lisa Tai

Picture Researcher Sophie Delpech
Production Controller Nigel Reed

Getty Images/16–17 /Sara Gray 106–107 /David Loftus 74–75
/Brian Stablyk 36–37 /Jonelle Weaver 88–89
Octopus Publishing Group Limited/Frank Adam 12
/Clive Bozzard-Hill 123 /Jean Cazals 28 /Stephen Conroy 112
/Gus Filgate 4, 44, 77, 103 /Jeremy Hopley 3, 5, 9, 49, 53, 65,
79, 81 /David Jordan 2, 6, 27, 47, 51, 91, 105 /William Lingwood
24, 29, 39, 59, 66, 69, 92, 97, 115, 121 /James Merrell 1, 19, 33,
41, 54–55, 86, 111, 117 /Hilary Moore 11 /Alan Newman 31
/Lis Parsons 95, 99, 118, 125 /William Reavell 100 /Gareth
Sambidge 20, 30, 35, 38, 43, 50, 57, 60, 63, 70, 73, 83, 85,
102, 109 /Ian Wallace 15, 23